a science unit for high-ability learners in grades 1–2

Budding Botanists

a science unit for high-ability learners in grades 1–2

Budding Botanists

WINNER: 2008 NAGC Curriculum Studies Award

Project Clarion Primary Science Units
Funded by the Jacob K. Javits Program, United States Department of Education

The College of William and Mary
School of Education
Center for Gifted Education
P.O. Box 8795
Williamsburg, VA 23187-8795

Co-Principal Investigators: Bruce A. Bracken & Joyce VanTassel-Baska
Project Directors: Lori C. Bland, Tamra Stambaugh, & Valerie Gregory
Unit Developers: Cindy Holub & Denise Drain
Unit Revision: Joyce VanTassel-Baska

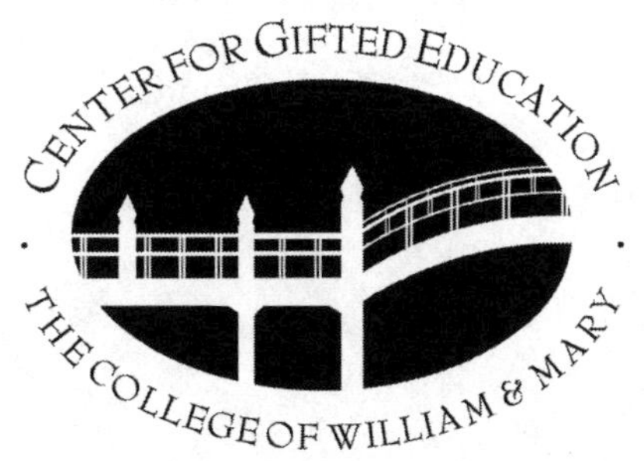

Edited by Lacy Compton
Production Design by Marjorie Parker

ISBN-13: 978-1-59363-386-8
ISBN-10: 1-59363-386-6

Prufrock Press Inc.
P.O. Box 8813
Waco, TX 76714-8813
Phone: (800) 998-2208
Fax: (800) 240-0333
http://www.prufrock.com

Contents

Part I: Unit Overview

Introduction to the Clarion Units

The Project Clarion Science Units for Primary Grades introduce young students to science concepts, science reasoning, and scientific investigative processes. Macroconcepts, such as systems or change, help students connect understanding of science content and processes. The units use a hands-on, constructivist approach that allows children to build their knowledge base and their skills as they explore science topics through play and planned investigations. Students are engaged in creative and critical thinking, problem finding and solving, process skill development, and communication opportunities. Conceptual understanding is reinforced as units strengthen basic language and mathematical concepts, including quantity, direction, position, comparison, colors, letter identification, numbers, counting, size, social awareness, texture, material, shape, time, and sequence.

Introduction to the *Budding Botanists* Unit

Budding Botanists, a first- and second-grade life science unit, engages students in a scenario-based approach to investigating plant life. The unit focuses on the macroconcept of systems to help students understand scientific systems such as plants and their components. The *Budding Botanists* unit builds upon students' prior knowledge of plant life and encourages them to use inquiry skills to observe, gather evidence, analyze data, and make inferences. The first lesson in this unit introduces students to the role of a scientist. Students assume the role of botanists working as a team to conduct investigations about plants. While working to understand the structure, nature, and life cycle of plants, the team members seek to answer questions such as "How can plants be used to fuel cars?"

Curriculum Framework

The curriculum framework (see Table 1) developed for the Project Clarion science units is based on the Integrated Curriculum Model (ICM), which posits the relatively equal importance of teaching to high-level content, higher order processes and resultant products, and important concepts and issues. The model represents a research-based set of differentiated curricular and instructional approaches found appropriate for high-ability learners (VanTassel-Baska, 1986; VanTassel-Baska & Little, 2003). The framework serves several important functions:

1. The curriculum framework provides scaffolding for the central concept of systems, the scientific research process, and the content of the units.
2. The curriculum framework also provides representative statements of advanced, complex, and sophisticated learner outcomes. It demonstrates how a single set of outcomes for all can be translated appropriately for high-ability learners, yet can remain accessible to other learners.
3. The curriculum framework provides a way for readers to get a snapshot view of the key emphases of the curriculum in direct relation to each other. The model also provides a way to traverse the elements individually through the continuum of grade levels.

Table 1
Project Clarion Curriculum Framework for Science Units

Goal	Student Outcomes The student will be able to:
1. Develop concepts related to understanding the world of science.	• Provide examples and salient features of various concepts. • Classify various concepts. • Identify counterexamples of various concepts. • Create definitions or generalizations about various concepts.
2. Develop an understanding of the macroconcept of systems as applied to science content goals.	• Identify the elements of a system. • Determine the boundaries of a system. • Label the inputs and the outputs of a system. • Analyze system interactions.
3. Develop knowledge of selected content topics in botany.	• Understand that plants have basic needs, including air, water, nutrients, and light. • Understand that different plant parts serve different functions in growth, survival, and reproduction. • Understand that plants undergo many changes during their life cycles. • Understand that different plants have different characteristics. • Understand that plants may cause changes in the environment where they live.
4. Develop interrelated science process skills.	• Make observations. • Ask questions. • Learn more. • Design and conduct experiments. • Create meaning. • Tell others what was found.
5. Develop critical thinking skills.	• Describe problematic situations or issues. • Define relevant concepts. • Identify different points of view in situations or issues. • Describe evidence or data supporting a scientific question. • Draw conclusions based on data (making inferences). • Predict consequences.
6. Develop creative thinking skills.	• Develop fluency when naming objects and ideas, based on a stimulus. • Develop flexible thinking. • Elaborate on ideas presented in oral or written form. • Create novel products.
7. Develop curiosity and interest in the world of science.	• Express reactions about discrepant events. • Ask meaningful questions about science topics. • Articulate ideas of interest about science. • Demonstrate persistence in completing science tasks.

Moreover, the framework may be used to implement the William and Mary units and to aid in new curriculum development based on science reform recommendations.

Standards Alignment

Each lesson was aligned to the appropriate National Science Education Standards (NSES), Content Standards: K–4 (Center for Science, Mathematics, and Engineering Education [CSMEE], 1996). Table 2 presents detailed information on the

Table 2

Budding Botanist Alignment to National Science Education Standards

Standard	Fundamental Concepts	Unit Lesson
Content Standard A: Abilities necessary to do scientific inquiry.	• Ask a question about objects, organisms, and events in the environment. • Plan and conduct a simple investigation. • Employ simple equipment and tools to gather data and extend the senses. • Use data to construct a reasonable explanation. • Communicate investigations and explanations.	1, 2, 3, 4, 5, 6, 7, 8, 9, 10, 11, 12, 13
Content Standard A: Understanding about scientific inquiry.	• Scientific investigations involve asking and answering a question and comparing the answer with what scientists already know about the world. • Scientists use different kinds of investigations, depending on the questions they are trying to answer. Types of investigations include: describing objects, events, and organisms; classifying them; and doing a fair test (experimenting). • Simple instruments, such as magnifiers, thermometers, and rulers, provide more information than scientists obtain using only their senses. • Scientists develop explanations using observations (evidence) and what they already know about the world (scientific knowledge). Good explanations are based on evidence from investigations. • Scientists make the results of their investigations public; they describe the investigation in ways that enable others to repeat the investigation. • Scientists review and ask questions about the results of other scientists' work.	1, 2, 3, 4, 5, 6, 7, 8, 9, 10, 11, 12, 13
Content Standard B: Properties of objects and materials.	• Objects have many observable properties, including size, weight, shape, color, temperature, and the ability to react with other substances. Those properties can be measured using tools, such as rulers, balances, and thermometers.	2, 3, 4, 5, 7, 8, 9, 10, 11, 12, 13
Content Standard C: The characteristics of organisms.	• Organisms have basic needs. For example, animals need air, water, and food; plants require air, water, nutrients, and light. Organisms can survive only in environments in which their needs can be met. The world has many different environments, and distinct environments support the life of different types of organisms. • Each plant or animal has different structures that serve different functions in growth, survival, and reproduction. For example, humans have distinct body structures for walking, holding, seeing, and talking.	2, 3, 4, 5, 7, 8, 9, 10, 11, 12, 13
Content Standard C: Life cycles of organisms.	• Plants and animals have life cycles that include being born, developing into adults, reproducing, and eventually dying. The details of this life cycle are different for different organisms.	4, 5, 7, 8, 9, 10, 11, 12, 13
Content Standard C: Organisms and environments.	• An organism's pattern of behavior is related to the nature of that organism's environment, including the kinds and numbers of other organisms present, the availability of food and resources, and the physical characteristics of the environment. When the environment changes, some plants and animals survive and reproduce and others die or move to a new location. • All organisms cause changes in the environment where they live. Some of these changes are detrimental to the organism or other organisms, whereas others are beneficial.	3, 8, 10, 11, 12, 13
Content Standard F: Science and technology in local challenges.	• People continue inventing new ways of doing things, solving problems, and getting work done. New ideas and inventions often affect other people; sometimes the effects are good and sometimes they are bad. It is helpful to try to determine in advance how ideas and inventions will affect other people. • Science and technology have greatly improved food quality and quantity, transportation, health, sanitation, and communication. These benefits of science and technology are not available to all people in the world.	6, 12, 13

alignment between the NSES Content Standards and fundamental concepts within the unit lessons.

Macroconcept

The macroconcept for this unit is *systems*. A concept paper on systems is included in Appendix A. The second lesson in this unit introduces the concept of systems. Students are asked to brainstorm examples of systems, categorize their examples, identify "nonexamples" of the concept, and make generalizations about the concept (Taba, 1962). The generalizations about systems incorporated into this unit of study include:

- Systems have parts (elements).
- Systems have boundaries.
- Systems may have inputs and outputs.
- A system's elements interact with each other and a system's inputs.

The concept of systems is integrated throughout the unit lessons and deepens students' understanding of plants, seeds, and even cells as systems. Students examine the relationship of important ideas and issues about plants through application of the concept generalizations. This higher level thinking enhances the students' ability to "think like a scientist." More information about concept development is provided in Appendix B: Teaching Models.

Key Science Concepts

By the end of this unit, students will understand that:

1. Plants have basic needs, including air, water, nutrients, and light.
2. Different parts of plants serve different functions in growth, survival, and reproduction.
3. Plants produce oxygen and food.
4. Plants are dependent on other living things and their surroundings for survival.
5. Plants undergo many changes during their life cycles.
6. Plants have different characteristics.
7. Plants cause changes in the environment where they live.

Practice in using concept maps supports students' learning as they begin to build upon known concepts (Novak & Gowin, 1984). Students begin to add new concepts to their initial understandings of a topic and to make new connections between concepts. The use of concept maps within the lessons also helps teachers to recognize students' conceptual frameworks so that instruction can be adapted as necessary. More information on strategies for using concept mapping, as well as a list of concept mapping practice activities, is provided in Appendix B.

Each Project Clarion unit contains a science concept map (see Figure 1) that displays the essential understandings and the connections students should be able to make as a result of their experiences within the unit. This overview may be useful as a classroom poster that teachers and students can refer to throughout the unit.

In addition to the concept map, teachers also will notice references to a "word wall" in the unit. The word wall is suggested for use in the classroom while teaching the unit. On this wall, teachers will post or write words (and their definitions) that go along with the lessons. Use the definitions listed in the Unit Glossary for the word wall; also use additional vocabulary from the lessons that may be unfamiliar to the students. At the end of the unit, teachers are instructed to assign words from the word wall to

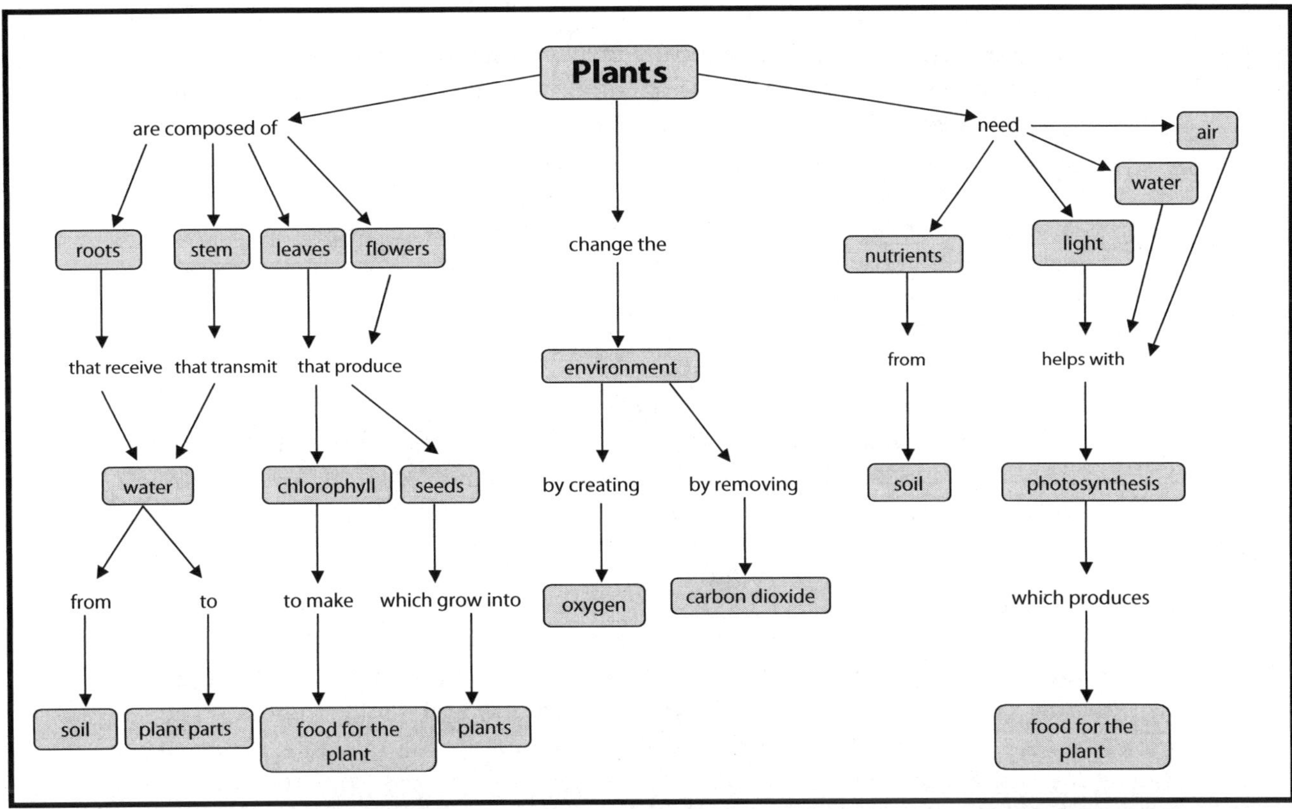

Figure 1. *Budding Botanists* unit concept map.

student groups for an activity that involves students creating word demonstrations. Teachers can assess students' understanding of each word or concept by the quality of understanding demonstrated in students' presentations.

Scientific Investigation and Reasoning

The Wheel of Scientific Investigation and Reasoning contains the specific processes involved in scientific inquiry that guide students' thinking and actions. To read more about these processes and suggestions for implementing the wheel into this unit's lessons, see Appendix B.

The lessons that utilize the Wheel of Scientific Investigation and Reasoning include:

- Lessons 4 and 5, which help students gain a better understanding of what scientists do and introduce the Wheel of Scientific Investigation and Reasoning. Students explore six components of scientific investigation including Make Observations, Ask Questions, Learn More, Design and Conduct Experiments, Create Meaning, and Share Results.
- Lessons 6–13, which provide opportunities for students to apply one or more components of scientific investigation and culminate with an in-depth scientific investigation.

Students use the wheel to analyze aspects of an investigation or to plan an investigation. Scientific investigation concepts within the lessons include:

- *Make Observations*: Scientists use their senses as well as instruments to note details, identify similarities and differences, and record changes in phenomena.

- *Ask Questions*: Scientists use information from their observations about familiar objects or events to develop important questions that spark further investigation.
- *Learn More*: Scientists carefully review what is known about a topic and determine what additional information must be sought.
- *Design and Conduct Experiments*: Scientists design an experiment, which is a fair test of a hypothesis or prediction and is intended to answer a question for a scientific investigation.
- *Create Meaning*: Scientists carefully gather and record data from an experiment, then analyze the data.
- *Share Results*: Scientists communicate findings from an experiment, including a clear description of the question, the hypothesis or prediction, the experiment that was conducted, the data that were collected and how they were analyzed, and the conclusions and inferences that were made from the experiment.

Assessment

The unit includes performance-based assessments for students to complete at the beginning (preassessment) and end (postassessment) of the unit. There are three pre- and postassessments, which assess conceptual understanding, science content knowledge, and application of the scientific investigation process. The preassessment provides baseline data that teachers can use to adjust instructional plans for individual students or groups of students. Preteaching activities accompany selected preassessments.

The postassessment is administered at the completion of the unit and provides valuable information about students' mastery of the targeted objectives and the National Science Education Standards. A rubric is used to score each pre- and postassessment. The pre- and postassessments and dimensions of learning scored for each task include:

- *A macroconcept template, which requires students to draw or write about the macroconcept.* Conceptual understanding is scored on the pre- and postassessments based on the number of appropriate examples of the macroconcept, the elements of the macroconcept, types of the macroconcept listed, and generalizations about the macroconcept.
- *Concept maps, which assess students' content knowledge.* Students are given a prompt for creating a concept map about the unit topic. Understanding of key science concepts is scored on the pre- and postassessments based on the number of appropriate hierarchical levels, propositions, and examples listed.
- *An experimental design template, which requires students to plan an experiment with a given scientific research question.* Students are asked to design an experiment to investigate a question. Students are scored on the pre- and postassessments on their ability to write a prediction or hypothesis, list materials needed for the experiment, list the steps of the experiment in order, and develop a plan to organize data for collection and interpretation.

Teachers also should note that assessment "Look Fors" are designated in the first section of each lesson plan. The "Look Fors" provide a means for teachers to assess student learning in each lesson. The "Look Fors" are linked to the macroconcept generalizations, key science concepts, and scientific processes identified in each lesson. Teachers can develop checklists for the "Look Fors" or may make informal observations.

Teacher's Guide to Content

The following definitions of key science concepts taught in the unit are described along with a list of content resources and a unit glossary.

Taxonomic Kingdoms

Early scientists divided the living world into plants and animals. Anything that moved under its own power was an animal; anything that did not was a plant. Later scientists realized that this division did not accurately reflect current knowledge of biology. Specifically, while the animal kingdom stayed virtually unchanged, scientists found that many organisms classified as plants were so different from each other that more kingdoms were needed to encompass the diversity of the early plant kingdom. Other kingdoms, such as fungi and protists, were added. Today, scientists use the term *plant* to refer to organisms with cell walls that use photosynthesis to manufacture energy from sunlight.

Structure of a Plant and Flower

Even plants as different from one another as a tulip and an oak tree share the same basic physical structure. Plants have two organ systems: the root system below ground and the stem system above ground. The root system anchors the plant into the ground and collects water and nutrients from the soil. The stem system includes the plant's stem and leaves, as well as fruit and flowers, if the plant has them. The plant's stem supports it and carries nutrients to all of its parts. The leaves manufacture food through photosynthesis. The flower and fruit are used in reproduction.

A flower has four main parts, arranged inside one another in rings. The outermost layer is called the sepal. The sepal protects the flower before it blooms. The petals are the second layer. They are generally brightly colored and prominent in insect-pollinated flowers. Flowers pollinated by wind have less prominent petals. Inside the petals are the flower's male and female reproductive structures. The stamen is the male structure, which produces pollen. The carpel, or female reproductive structure, produces fruit after pollination.

Plant and Animal Cells

Plant and animal cells share many similarities, including the presence of a nucleus that controls the workings of the cell and other organelles, or structures with a specialized function within a cell. Despite these similarities, there are two important differences between plant and animal cells. First, plant cells are surrounded by a cell wall made of cellulose fibers. The cell wall gives the plant structure, allowing the plant to grow tall without a skeletal system to lend support. Cellulose is useful to people as well; we use cellulose fibers to make paper, fabric, and other products. Second, plant cells have special organelles called *chloroplasts*. Chloroplasts are necessary for photosynthesis.

The following content notes should be reviewed before teaching Lesson 10.

Photosynthesis, Respiration, and Transpiration

In order for a plant to grow and develop, three processes must occur in balance: photosynthesis, respiration, and transpiration. These three processes are responsible for creating carbohydrates the plant will use as food and energy; breaking down the created carbohydrates into usable energy; and transporting minerals, sugars, and other plant chemicals through the plant.

Photosynthesis

Photosynthesis is the process by which a plant converts sunlight, carbon dioxide, and water into food. The plant gathers and stores sunlight using chloroplasts, which trap sunlight using chlorophyll. Chlorophyll is the pigment or chemical that gives plants their green color. Chlorophyll can absorb red and blue light but not green light. Because green light is not absorbed, it is reflected, which causes the plant to appear green. This stored light is used as energy in the process of converting carbon dioxide from the air and water from the soil into carbohydrates or sugars. The stored energy is used to split the carbon dioxide into carbon and oxygen. Carbohydrates occur when the carbon is then combined with water. These carbohydrates are converted into usable energy through respiration, stored, or combined to create more complex energy compounds such as oils and proteins. The formula for photosynthesis is written as:

carbon dioxide + water + sunlight = sugar + oxygen
The chemical formula is:
$6CO_2 + 6H_2O + \text{light energy} = C_6H_{12}O_6 + 6O_2$

Respiration

Respiration is the process of turning the carbohydrates and sugars created from photosynthesis into usable energy. This process also is called *controlled oxidation*. Controlled oxidation is similar to oxidation that occurs when burning wood to create heat. It also is the opposite process of photosynthesis. The process of photosynthesis creates a more complex molecule, while the process of respiration breaks down a complex molecule into simpler molecules. During respiration, carbohydrates and oxygen are combined to create carbon dioxide, water, and usable energy. All life forms and cells depend on respiration. Respiration occurs at all times and is not dependent on sunlight so it also occurs at night. The chemical formula for respiration is:

$C_6H_{12}O_6 + 6O_2 = 6CO_2 + 6H_2O + \text{energy (36 ATP)}$

Transpiration

Transpiration is the loss of water to the atmosphere through the plant's leaves, which are covered with little openings called *stomata*. The plant controls the opening and closing of the stomata. As the stomata open, water and oxygen are released into the atmosphere. At the same time, the plant brings in carbon dioxide, which it needs for photosynthesis. This process also is used to bring nutrients and water from the soil into the roots of the plant and then carry them throughout the entire plant. As water is lost to the atmosphere, more water is pulled up from the roots and carried through the plant. The rate of transpiration of a plant is dependent on temperature, humidity, and wind. The greatest amount of transpiration would take place in an environment that has a high temperature, has low humidity, and is windy.

All three processes—photosynthesis, respiration, and transpiration—are interrelated. Photosynthesis must occur in order to create carbohydrates, which then are broken down into usable energy during respiration. If transpiration does not occur, then CO_2 is not brought into the plant and photosynthesis cannot occur. If respiration does not occur, then the plant cells do not have enough energy to function or grow and plant growth will stop. If photosynthesis does not occur, then the plant will not have any food sources and will die. Therefore, all three processes must occur in balance in order for the plant to grow and develop correctly.

Unit Glossary

Carbon dioxide: A gas in the air that is made up of carbon and oxygen. People and animals breathe out carbon dioxide, while plants absorb it during the day.

Cell: The basic, microscopic unit of all living things.

Cell membrane: A thin layer regulating what goes in and out of a cell.

Cell wall: A thick layer of fiber that surrounds a plant cell and provides support to the cell.

Chlorophyll: The green substance in plants that uses light to manufacture food from carbon dioxide and water.

Chloroplast: The site of photosynthesis in plants, the chloroplast makes sugar (glucose) and oxygen.

Chromatography: The process of separating parts of a mixture by letting it travel through a material that absorbs each part at a different rate.

Flower: The colored part of a plant that produces seeds and sometimes fruit.

Leaf: A flat, usually green, part of a plant that makes food by the process of photosynthesis and gives off oxygen as a by-product.

Mitochondria: The part of a cell that helps make an energy molecule called ATP.

Nitrogen: A colorless, odorless gas that makes up about 80% of the Earth's air.

Nucleus: The brain of the cell, it tells the cell what to do.

Nutrient: A substance that is needed by people, animals, and plants to stay strong and healthy. Proteins, minerals, and vitamins are all nutrients.

Oxygen: A colorless, odorless gas found in air that makes up about 21% of the Earth's atmosphere. Humans and other animals need oxygen to breathe.

Photosynthesis: A chemical process by which green plants make their food. Plants use energy from the sun to turn water and carbon dioxide into food, and they give off oxygen as a by-product.

Pollen: Tiny yellow grains produced in the anthers of flowers. Pollen grains are the male cells of flowering plants.

Reproduction: The process by which living things give rise to new living things of the same species.

Respiration: A chemical process by which plants use oxygen from the air and the energy they have stored to make carbon dioxide and water. It is the opposite of photosynthesis.

Root: The part of a plant or tree that grows underground.

Seed: The part of a flowering plant from which a new plant can grow.

Seed coat: The outer covering of a seed.

Sprout: A new or young plant growth.

Stem: The long main part of a plant from which the leaves and flowers grow.

Teaching Resources

Required Resources (Used in Relevant Lessons)

Lehn, B. (1999). *What is a scientist?* Minneapolis, MN: Millbrook Press.

Additional Resources

Arbel, I. (2004). *Amazing plants.* Mineola, NY: Dover.
Bates, T. (1994). *Flowers and seeds.* Greensboro, NC: Carson-Dellosa.
Dow, L., Carolin, R. C., & Addario, S. (1997). *Incredible plants.* Alexandria, VA: Time-Life Books.
Gardiner, J. R. (1995). *Top secret.* New York: Little, Brown.
Goldner, K. (1996). *Plants in our world.* Nashua, NH: Delta Education.
Heller, R. (1999). *The reason for a flower.* New York: Penguin Putnam.
Jordan, H. J., & Krupinski, L. (1992). *How a seed grows.* New York: HarperCollins.
Padilla, M. J., Miaoulis, I., & Cyr, M. (2007). *Science explorer: From bacteria to plants.* Upper Saddle River, NJ: Prentice Hall.
Robbins, K. (2005). *Seeds.* New York: Atheneum.
Silverstein, A., Silverstein V. B., & Nunn, L. S. (2007). *Photosynthesis.* Minneapolis, MN: Twenty-First Century Books.
VanCleave, J. (1990). *Janice VanCleave's biology for every kid.* Indianapolis, IN: Wiley.

Useful Web Sites

A to Z Home's Cool Homeschooling. (n.d.). *Plant science projects for kids.* Retrieved March 26, 2009, from http://homeschooling.gomilpitas.com/explore/botany.htm
American Society of Plant Biologists. (n.d.). *Principles of plant biology.* Retrieved March 26, 2009, from http://www.aspb.org/education/foundation/principles.cfm
Andrew Rader Studios. (n.d.). *Biology for kids.* Retrieved March 26, 2009, from http://www.biology4kids.com/files/plants_main.html
Carter, J. S. (1996). *Photosynthesis.* Retrieved March 26, 2009, from http://biology.clc.uc.edu/courses/bio104/photosyn.htm
Farabee, M. J. (2007). *Photosynthesis.* Retrieved March 26, 2009, from http://www.emc.maricopa.edu/faculty/farabee/BIOBK/BioBookPS.html
KIdsBIology.com (n.d.). *What is biology?.* Retrieved March 26, 2009, from http://www.kidsbiology.com/biology_basics
Kids Online Resources. (n.d.). *Science: Botany, Pg: 1 of 2.* Retrieved March 26, 2009, from http://www.kidsolr.com/science/page9.html
Kids' Turn Central. (n.d.). *Science resources—Botany.* Retrieved March 26, 2009, from http://www.kidsturncentral.com/links/botanylinks.htm
Kimball, J. (2006). *The plant cell.* Retrieved March 26, 2009, from http://users.rcn.com/jkimball.ma.ultranet/BiologyPages/P/PlantCell.html
Knee, M. (n.d.). *Plant cells.* Retrieved March 26, 2009, from http://www.hcs.ohio-state.edu/hcs300/cell1.htm
National Science Foundation. (2008). *Biology classroom resources.* Retrieved March 26, 2009, from http://www.nsf.gov/news/classroom/biology.jsp

Oregon State University. (1999). *Plant growth and development—Photosynthesis, respiration, transpiration.* Retrieved March 26, 2009, from http://extension.oregonstate.edu/mg/botany/growth.html

Science.gov. (May 2008). *Resources for kids, parents and teachers.* Retrieved March 26, 2009, from http://www.science.gov/browse/w_133A.htm

Soltis, P., Soltis, D., & Edwards, C. (2005). *Angiosperms: Flowering plants.* Retrieved March 26, 2009, from http://tolweb.org/tree?group=angiosperms

University of Illinois Extension. (n.d.). *The great plant escape.* Retrieved March 26, 2009, from http://www.urbanext.uiuc.edu/gpe/gpe.html

University of Michigan. (n.d.). *A primer on photosynthesis and the functioning of cells.* Retrieved March 26, 2009, from http://www.globalchange.umich.edu/globalchange1/current/lectures/kling/energyflow/PSN_primer.html

Part II: Lesson Plans

Lesson Plans

Overview of Lessons

Preteaching Lesson: Science Safety

Preassessment

Lesson 1: What Is a Scientist?

Lesson 2: What Is a System?

Lesson 3: Terrariums as Systems

Lesson 4: What Scientists Do—Observe, Question, Learn More

Lesson 5: What Scientists Do—Experiment, Create Meaning, Tell Others

Lesson 6: A Real-World Problem to Solve!

Lesson 7: Animal, Vegetable, or Mineral: What Is It?

Lesson 8: Close Up: Using a Microscope

Lesson 9: Just a Little Seed

Lesson 10: Plant Experimentation on Basic Needs

Lesson 11: Follow-Up to Plant Experiments

Lesson 12: Independent and Small-Group Investigation

Lesson 13: Wrap It Up!

Postassessment

Table 3
Overview of Lessons

Concept of Systems	Scientific Process	Key Science Concepts
	Preassessment	
	Lesson 1: What Is a Scientist?	
Lesson 2: What Is a System?		
Lesson 3: Terrariums as Systems		
	Lesson 4: What Scientists Do—Observe, Question, Learn More	
	Lesson 5: What Scientists Do—Experiment, Create Meaning, Tell Others	
	Lesson 6: A Real-World Problem to Solve!	
Lesson 7: Animal, Vegetable, or Mineral: What Is It?		Lesson 7: Animal, Vegetable, or Mineral: What Is It?
		Lesson 8: Close Up: Using a Microscope
	Lesson 9: Just a Little Seed	
		Lesson 10: Plant Experimentation on Basic Needs
		Lesson 11: Follow-Up to Plant Experiments
	Lesson 12: Independent and Small-Group Investigation	Lesson 12: Independent and Small-Group Investigation
	Lesson 13: Wrap It Up!	
	Postassessment	

Overview of Lessons

An overview of the lessons is provided in Table 3. The overview shows the primary emphasis of each lesson in the unit according to the macroconcept, key science concepts, or the scientific investigative process. Lessons also may have a secondary emphasis, which is listed in the planning section of each lesson, labeled "Planning the Lesson."

Lesson Plan Blueprint

The lesson plan blueprint (see Table 4) shows for each lesson:

- the instructional purpose,
- generalizations about the macroconcept of systems,
- key science concepts,
- scientific investigation skills and processes, and
- assessment "Look Fors."

Table 4
Lesson Plan Blueprint

Lesson Number	Title	Instructional Purposes	Systems Generalizations	Key Science Concepts	Scientific Investigation Skills and Processes	Assessment "Look Fors" Students should be able to:
	Preassessment					
1	What Is a Scientist?	• To learn the characteristics of scientists and investigation skills that scientists use.			• Make observations. • Ask questions. • Learn more. • Design and conduct experiments. • Create meaning. • Tell others what was found.	• Identify scientific investigation processes used by scientists.
2	What Is a System?	• To review the concept preassessment with the class. • To introduce the concept of systems. • To apply understandings about systems to a new system.	• Systems have parts (elements). • Systems have boundaries. • Systems have inputs and outputs. • A system's elements interact with each other and a system's inputs.			• Describe a system.
3	Terrariums as Systems	• To apply the concept of systems to a terrarium. • To make generalizations about the terrarium as a system.	• Systems have parts (elements). • Systems have boundaries. • Systems have inputs and outputs. • A system's elements interact with each other and a system's inputs.	• Plants have basic needs, including air, water, nutrients, and light. • Plants are dependent on other living things and their surroundings for survival. • Plants cause changes in the environment where they live. • Plants produce oxygen and food.		• Describe a terrarium as a system.
4	What Scientists Do—Observe, Question, Learn More	• To introduce the Wheel of Scientific Investigation and Reasoning. • To introduce how to conduct an experiment by making observations about flower petals. • To observe seeds and how they change over time.	• Systems have parts (elements). • Systems have boundaries.	• Plants have different parts that serve different functions in growth, survival, and reproduction.	• Make observations. • Ask questions. • Learn more. • Design and conduct experiments. • Create meaning. • Tell others what was found.	• Apply the steps of scientific investigation. • Interpret data from a data table.
5	What Scientists Do—Experiment, Create Meaning, Tell Others	• To continue using the Wheel of Scientific Investigation and Reasoning. • To observe seeds and how they change over time.	• Systems have parts (elements). • Systems have boundaries. • Systems have inputs and outputs. • A system's elements interact with each other and a system's inputs.	• Plants have different parts that serve different functions in growth, survival, and reproduction.	• Make observations. • Ask questions. • Learn more. • Design and conduct experiments. • Create meaning. • Tell others what was found.	• Apply the steps of scientific investigation. • Interpret data from a data table. • Describe how the experiment was conducted and what results were found.

Lesson Number	Title	Instructional Purposes	Systems Generalizations	Key Science Concepts	Scientific Investigation Skills and Processes	Assessment "Look Fors" Students should be able to:
6	A Real-World Problem to Solve!	• To use the scientific process skills of observing, collecting data, and making inferences. • To understand that locating resources is an important part of "learning more."			• Make observations. • Ask questions. • Learn more. • Create meaning.	• Ask questions about the message and log entry. • Generate ideas for the Need to Know Board.
7	Animal, Vegetable, or Mineral: What Is It?	• To understand the distinguishing characteristics and qualities of plants.	• Systems have parts (elements). • Systems have boundaries. • Systems have inputs and outputs. • A system's elements interact with each other and a system's inputs.	• Plants have basic needs, including air, water, nutrients, and light. • Plants have different parts that serve different functions in growth, survival, and reproduction. • Different plants have different characteristics.	• Make observations. • Learn more. • Create meaning.	• Use correct definitions for plants. • Apply generalizations about systems to plants.
8	Close Up: Using a Microscope	• To investigate and understand basic plant anatomy, including the nature of plant cells through use of a microscope.	• Systems have parts (elements). • Systems have boundaries. • Systems have inputs and outputs. • A system's elements interact with each other and a system's inputs.	• Plants have different parts that serve different functions in growth, survival, and reproduction. • Different plants have different characteristics.	• Make observations. • Learn more. • Create meaning.	• Record observations from slides and apply labels appropriately. • Handle the microscopes correctly.
9	Just a Little Seed	• To create a mini greenhouse using zipper bags to germinate seeds. • To observe and document seed development and growth. • To dissect seeds and identify seed parts.	• Systems have parts (elements). • Systems have boundaries. • Systems have inputs and outputs. • A system's elements interact with each other and a system's inputs.	• Plants have different parts that serve different functions in growth, survival, and reproduction. • Plants undergo many changes during their life cycles.	• Make observations. • Ask questions. • Learn more. • Design and conduct experiments. • Create meaning. • Tell others what was found.	• Look at a dissected seed, point to the parts of the seed, name the parts, and explain the function.
10	Plant Experimentation on Basic Needs	• To investigate and understand basic plant life processes. • To demonstrate an understanding of plant system interactions.	• Systems have parts (elements). • Systems have boundaries. • Systems have inputs and outputs. • A system's elements interact with each other and a system's inputs.	• Plants have basic needs, including air, water, nutrients, and light. • Plants are dependent on other living things and their surroundings for survival. • Plants have different parts that serve different functions in growth, survival, and reproduction. • Plants undergo many changes during their life cycles.	• Make observations. • Ask questions. • Learn more. • Design and conduct experiments. • Create meaning. • Tell others what was found.	• Record a hypothesis or prediction. • Identify materials used to test a hypothesis. • Outline and follow steps to test a hypothesis. • Make observations and record data. • Determine whether the hypothesis was proven and describe the findings. • Identify new questions.

Lesson Number	Title	Instructional Purposes	Systems Generalizations	Key Science Concepts	Scientific Investigation Skills and Processes	Assessment "Look Fors" Students should be able to:
11	Follow-Up to Plant Experiments	• To share results of plant experiments.	• Systems have parts (elements). • Systems have boundaries. • Systems have inputs and outputs. • A system's elements interact with each other and a system's inputs.	• Plants have basic needs, including air, water, nutrients, and light. • Plants are dependent on other living things and their surroundings for survival. • Plants have different parts that serve different functions in growth, survival, and reproduction. • Plants undergo many changes during their life cycles.	• Create meaning. • Tell others what was found.	• Articulate findings. • Show understanding of science investigation skills and processes. • Discuss plants as systems.
12	Independent and Small-Group Investigation	• To share student projects on seeds. • To share resolutions to Professor Blackwell's work on using plants for fuel.	• Systems have parts (elements). • Systems have boundaries. • Systems have inputs and outputs. • A system's elements interact with each other and a system's inputs.	• Plants have different parts that serve different functions in growth, survival, and reproduction. • Plants undergo many changes during their life cycles.	• Make observations. • Ask questions. • Learn more. • Design and conduct experiments. • Create meaning. • Tell others what was found.	• Share knowledge and understanding about their seed collection. • Make accurate inferences about whether plants can be used to fuel cars.
13	Wrap It Up!	• To summarize content, scientific process, and conceptual understanding.	• Systems have parts (elements). • Systems have boundaries. • Systems have inputs and outputs. • A system's elements interact with each other and a system's inputs.	• Plants have basic needs, including air, water, nutrients, and light. • Plants have different parts that serve different functions in growth, survival, and reproduction. • Plants undergo many changes during their life cycles. • Different plants have different characteristics. • Plants cause changes in the environment where they live.	• Make observations. • Ask questions. • Learn more. • Design and conduct experiments. • Create meaning. • Tell others what was found.	• Draw a concept map for a term in the unit. • Describe the scientific investigative process and explain its application to plants. • Describe a plant system.
	Postassessment					

Preteaching Lesson: Science Safety

Planning the Lesson

> **Note to Teacher**
> Please read Science Safety Guidelines (Handout 0A) prior to teaching this lesson.

Instructional Purpose

- To instill in students the importance of safety in the classroom.
- To outline science safety rules to be implemented throughout the unit.

Instructional Time

- 45 minutes

Materials/Resources/Equipment

- Sample materials:
  - Plant
  - Plastic bag of nonhazardous powdery substance (e.g., sugar)
  - Closed jar of nonhazardous liquid (e.g., water)

- Plastic disposable gloves
- Safety goggles
- Chart paper
- Markers
- Handout 0A (Science Safety Guidelines) for your review
- Poster of Handout 0B (Science Safety Rules)

Implementing the Lesson

1. Display sample materials on a long table in front of students. Inform students that they soon will begin a science unit in which they will observe and study many different kinds of materials, such as these. Explain that it is important for students to practice safety during the investigations. Relate the necessity of science safety rules to those of the classroom and physical education.
2. Display and define each item. Tell students that as a class they will create a list of rules they should follow when handling these materials. Have students think of how they can keep their bodies safe. Record these examples on chart paper.
3. Next, unveil the Science Safety Rules (Handout 0B) on chart paper. Have students compare this list to their own rules. How do students' examples relate to these rules? If necessary, add additional rules to the list.
4. Explain why some materials (such as knives) or elements (such as fire) are never appropriate for children to handle in school. Briefly discuss the potential hazards associated with these.
5. Finally, conduct a brief demonstration to illustrate how to practice safety guidelines. Take the plastic bag containing a nonhazardous powdery substance and the jar of nonhazardous liquid. Explain that you are going to investigate how the two materials interact. Ask students how you can be safe while doing this investigation. Reinforce that substances can be harmful to the eyes or skin and that they should **never** be ingested. Explain that the same is

true of plants, which can be toxic to humans. Emphasize that students should follow similar guidelines when studying plants.

6. Following students' examples of safety measures, demonstrate how to use safety goggles to protect the eyes, plastic gloves to protect the hands, and other relevant protective measures, such as pulling long hair back and wearing appropriate clothing. Conduct the demonstration by carefully pouring the powdery substance into the jar of liquid. Emphasize that you should never touch your face or mouth (and especially should not eat or drink) during science experiments.
7. Tell students that the teacher will dispose of materials properly after the investigation is completed. Students should not touch any potentially harmful substances.
8. Demonstrate the final rule, "Wash your hands," by properly removing the gloves (without the outside of the gloves ever touching the body) and the goggles. If there is a sink in the classroom, demonstrate how to properly wash one's hands. If no sink is present, inform students that after each investigation the class will go to the bathroom to wash their hands.
9. Conclude the lesson by emphasizing that science investigations are interesting and fun, but they also can be dangerous if not conducted properly. By following the Science Safety Rules, the class will enjoy the benefits of learning about science.

Handout 0A
Science Safety Guidelines

1. Know and follow your school's policies and procedures regarding classroom safety.
2. Always provide direct adult supervision when students are engaging in scientific experimentation.
3. Ensure that all materials and equipment are safe for handling by primary students.
4. Exert extra caution when materials have the potential for harm when used improperly.
5. Use protective gear for eyes, skin, and breathing when conducting experiments, and require students to do the same.
6. Always conduct an experiment by yourself before completing it with the students.
7. Store materials for experiments out of the reach of students.
8. Never allow students to eat or drink during science experiments.
9. Follow general safety rules for sharp objects, heated items, breakables, or spilled liquids.
10. Teach students that it is unsafe to touch their face, mouth, eyes, or other body parts when they are working with plants, animals, microorganisms, or chemicals. Wash hands prior to touching anything. Caution students about putting anything in their mouth or breathing in the smell of substances.
11. Be aware of students' allergies to plants, including plant pollen, animals, foods, chemicals, or other substances to be used in the science classroom. Take all precautions necessary. Common food allergens include peanuts, tree nuts (cashews, almonds, walnuts, hazelnuts, macadamia nuts, pecans, pistachios, and pine nuts), shellfish, fish, milk, eggs, wheat, and soy.
12. Use caution with plants. Never allow students to pick or handle any unknown plants, leaves, flowers, seeds, or berries. Use gloves to touch unknown plants. Many common house, garden, and wooded area plants are toxic.
13. Avoid glass jars and containers. Use plastic, paper, or cloth containers.
14. Thermometers should be filled with alcohol, not mercury.
15. Clearly label any chemicals used and dispose of properly.
16. Teach students safety rules for science (see Handout 0B), including:
    a. **Always** do scientific experiments with an adult present.
    b. **Never** mix things together (liquids, powders) without adult approval.
    c. **Use** your senses carefully. Protect your eyes, ears, nose, mouth, and skin.
    d. **Wash your hands** after using materials for an experiment.

Handout 0B

Science Safety Rules

1 **Always** do scientific experiments with an adult present.

2 **Never** mix things together (liquids, powders) without adult approval.

3 **Use** your senses carefully. Protect your eyes, ears, nose, mouth, and skin.

4 **Wash your hands** after using materials for an experiment.

Preassessment

Planning the Lesson

Instructional Purpose

- To determine prior knowledge of unit content.
- To build understanding of the unit concept, processes, and content.

Instructional Time

- Macroconcept assessment: 20 minutes
- Science content assessment: 30 minutes, including preteaching activity
- Scientific process assessment: 20 minutes

Materials/Resources/Equipment

- Copies of preassessments (Preassessment for Systems Concept, Preassessment for Science Content, Preassessment for Scientific Process) for each student
- Copy of blank Concept Map drawing sheet for each student
- Preteaching for Science Content instructions for your use
- Rubrics (Scoring Rubric for Systems Concept, Scoring Rubric for Science Content, Scoring Rubric for Scientific Process) for your use
- Pencils
- Large chart paper
- Drawing paper for each student

Implementing the Lesson

1. Each assessment should be administered on a different day.
2. Explain to students that the class is beginning a new unit of study. Tell them that they will be completing a preassessment to determine what they already know about the topic. Assure them that the assessment is not for a grade and encourage them to do their best. Use the preteaching instructions before administering the Preassessment for Science Content.
3. Collect all of the preassessments. Briefly review each assessment and discuss some of the responses in general, indicating that this unit will provide them with more knowledge and skills than they now have.
4. Score the preassessments using the rubrics provided. Keep the scores and assessments for diagnostic purposes to organize groups for various activities during the unit and to compare pre- and postassessment results.

Name:________________________________ Date:____________

Preassessment for Systems Concept

1. Give *five* examples of things that are "systems."

____

____

____

____

____

2. Draw *one* example of a system that you know.

3. Label at least *five* features of your system.

4. What are *three* things you can say about *all* systems?

All systems ____ .

All systems ____ .

All systems ____ .

Name:______________________________ Date:______________

Rubric 1
Scoring Rubric for Systems Concept

Directions for Use: Score students on their responses to each of the questions.

	5	4	3	2	1
Examples of the Macroconcept	Five or more appropriate examples are given.	Four appropriate examples are given.	Three appropriate examples are given.	Two appropriate examples are given.	One appropriate example is given.
Drawing of the Macroconcept	The drawing contains a recognizable system, with functioning parts.	The drawing contains most of the major elements of the system.	The drawing contains some elements of the system.	The drawing contains a few elements of the system.	The drawing contains only one element.
Features of the Macroconcept	The drawing contains at least five elements or other features of a system.	The drawing contains at least four elements or other features of a system.	The drawing contains at least three elements or other features of a system.	The drawing contains at least two elements or other features of a system.	The drawing contains at least one element or other feature of a system.
Generalization About the Macroconcept	Three appropriate generalizations are made about systems.	Three somewhat appropriate generalizations are made about systems.	Two appropriate generalizations are made about systems.	One appropriate generalization is made about systems.	Only a statement about systems is made.

Total points possible: 20

Preteaching for Science Content Preassessment

Directions for Use: Say the following bolded directions to students. Directions for you are not bolded.

Sometimes we know a lot about something even before our teachers teach it in school. Sometimes we don't know very much at all, but we like to learn new things.

For example, what would you think about if someone asked you to tell all you know about how *farms* work? What are some of the words you would use?

(List these on a chart.)

What are some of the things that happen on a farm?

(List these on a chart.)

I am going to show you a way I might tell all I know about how farms work.

(Begin a concept map on a large sheet of paper, using pictures and words, making simple links, and emphasizing these links; see Figure 2 for an example)

Make your own maps on your drawing paper. This practice activity can be done with a partner.

(Share some of the resulting concept maps, encouraging students to articulate their links.)

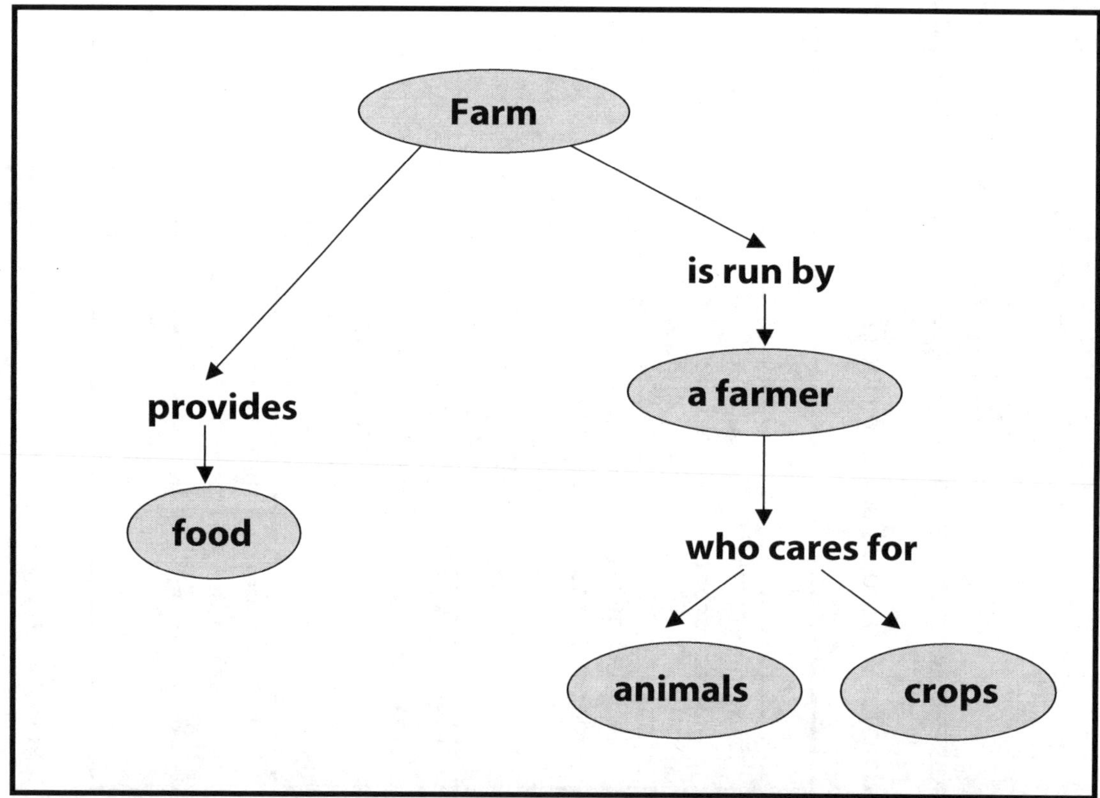

Figure 2. Concept map of farm.

Preassessment for Science Content

Directions for Use: Read the following paragraph to the students.

Today I would like you to think about all the things you know about plants. Think about the words you would use and the pictures you could draw to make a concept map. Think about the connections you can make. On your concept map paper, draw in pictures and words all that you know about plants. You will be drawing a concept map, just like the concept map you did when we discussed the farm. Today's instruction is: "Tell me everything you know about plants."

Name:________________________ Date:____________

Concept Map
Plants

Name:_______________ Date:_______________

Rubric 2
Scoring Rubric for Science Content

Directions for Use: Score students on their completed maps.

	5	4	3	2	1	0
Hierarchical Level Each subordinate concept is more specific and less general than the concept drawn above it. Count the number of levels included in the total map.	Five or more levels are identified.	Four levels are identified.	Three levels are identified.	Two levels are identified.	One level is identified.	No hierarchical levels are identified.
Propositions The linking of two concepts indicating a clear relationship is given. Count the total number of propositions identified on the total map.	Twelve or more propositions are provided.	Ten to twelve propositions are provided.	Seven to nine propositions are provided.	Four to six propositions are provided.	One to three propositions are provided.	No propositions are provided.
Examples A valid example of a concept is provided. Count the total number of examples.	Twelve or more examples are provided.	Ten to twelve examples are provided.	Seven to nine examples are provided.	Four to six examples are provided.	One to three examples are provided.	No examples are provided.

Total points possible: 15

Name:______________________________ Date:____________

Preassessment for Scientific Process

Directions: How would you study the question: Are plants attracted to the sun? Describe an experiment to test this question that includes the following:

1. Prediction regarding the question (Are plants attracted to the sun?):

   I predict that____

   ____

   ____

   ____.

2. What materials will be needed to conduct the experiment?

   ____________________ ____________________

   ____________________ ____________________

   ____________________ ____________________

3. What steps must be taken to conduct the experiment and *in what order*?

   a. ____

   b. ____

   c. ____

   d. ____

   e. ____

4. What data do you want to collect and how should the data be recorded?

What will I collect?	How will I record the data?

5. How do the data help me decide if my prediction is correct? Explain.

____

____

____

____

Name:________________________ Date:______________

Rubric 3

Scoring Rubric for Scientific Process

Directions for Use: Score students on the responses to each of the questions.

	Criteria	Strong Evidence 3	Some Evidence 2	Little Evidence 1	No Evidence 0
1	**Generates a Prediction**	Clearly generates a prediction appropriate to the experiment.	Somewhat generates a prediction appropriate to the experiment.	Generates an inappropriate prediction.	Fails to generate a prediction.
2	**Lists Materials Needed**	Provides an inclusive and appropriate list of materials.	Provides a partial list of materials needed.	Provides inappropriate materials.	Fails to provide a list of materials needed.
3	**Lists Experiment's Steps**	Clearly and concisely lists four or more steps as appropriate for the experiment design.	Clearly and concisely lists one to three steps as appropriate for the experiment design.	Generates inappropriate steps.	Fails to generate steps.
4	**Arranges Steps in Sequential Order**	Lists steps in sequential order.	Lists most of the steps or one step out of order.	Lists one or two steps or steps are placed in an illogical order.	Does not list steps.
5	**Plans Data Collection**	Clearly states a plan for data collection, including what data will be needed and how they will be recorded.	States a partial plan for data collection, citing some items for collection and some way of recording data.	Provides minimal plan for either data collection and/or recording.	Fails to identify any part of a plan for data collection.
6	**States Plan for Interpreting Data for Making Predictions**	Clearly states plan for interpreting data by linking data to prediction.	States a partial plan for interpreting data that links data to prediction.	Provides a brief statement that partially addresses use of data for prediction.	Fails to state plan for using data for making a prediction.

Total points possible: 18

Note. Adapted from Fowler (1990).

Lesson 1: What Is a Scientist?

Planning the Lesson

Instructional Purpose

- To learn the characteristics of scientists and the investigation skills that scientists use.

Instructional Time

- 45 minutes

Scientific Investigation Skills and Processes

- Make observations.
- Ask questions.
- Learn more.
- Design and conduct experiments.
- Create meaning.
- Tell others what was found.

Assessment "Look Fors"

- Students should be able to identify the scientific investigation processes used by scientists.

Materials/Resources/Equipment

- Lab coat for teacher
- One lab coat (white adult T-shirt or dress shirt) for each student
- Beaker
- Microscope or magnifying glass
- Prepared charts for students, PowerPoint slides, or transparencies of Handout 1A (Defining Scientists) and Handout 1B (What Scientists Do: The Wheel of Scientific Investigation and Reasoning)
- Chart of The Wheel of Scientific Investigation and Reasoning
- Marker
- One piece of chart paper
- Student log books
- *What Is a Scientist?* by Barbara Lehn

Implementing the Lesson

1. Put on a lab coat and pick up a beaker and microscope or magnifying glass. Ask the students what kind of job you might have. Explain that you are a scientist. Ask the students if they know a scientist and allow them to discuss what they know about scientists or their experiences with scientists. Record student responses to the following questions (you may wish to refer to the Frayer Model of Vocabulary Development in Appendix B):
   - Do you know a scientist?
   - What do you think scientists do?

2. Define a scientist as "a person who studies nature and the physical world by testing, experimenting, and measuring" (Scholastic, 1996) using the Defining Scientists sheet (Handout 1A).
3. Ask the students what they think scientists do and write down their responses on chart paper. Display the chart for What Scientists Do: The Wheel of Scientific Investigation and Reasoning (Handout 1B). Read the wheel to the students and talk about what each item means. Ask the students to compare the "What Scientists Do" processes with the list the class created.
4. Show students the book, *What Is a Scientist?* by Barbara Lehn. Ask students to look for what scientists do while you are reading the book. Read the book, showing the pictures to the students and pointing out the clues that will help students understand what a scientist does. As you read each page, relate the activity to the scientific investigation processes included on the wheel. Ask students these questions:
    - What did the scientists do in the book?
    - What makes someone a scientist?
    - When is someone *not* a scientist?

5. Explain that the students will be working as scientists in the unit. Have students put on their "lab coats." Explain to the students that they are going to learn to think like a scientist and learn how to do what scientists do.
6. Tell students that scientists keep a scientific investigation log of what they are doing. They date the pages in their logs and then write down what they have learned or what they are thinking about what they learned. Tell students that they are going to keep a log, and they are going to make the first page now. Pass out student log books. Ask each student to date the first page and to draw a picture of him- or herself investigating something as a scientist.
7. Have students share their completed pictures with the class.
8. Concluding questions:
    - Would you like to be a scientist? Why or why not?
    - All science is about how things stay the same and how they change. How do scientists study change?

Concluding and Extending the Lesson

- Provide "props" and "lab coats" for students to role-play being a scientist in the housekeeping section of the classroom.
- Provide books about individuals who are investigating something in the library center of the classroom.

What to Do at Home

- Ask students to ask their parent or some other adult to respond to the question: "What would you investigate/study/do if you were a scientist?"

Handout 1A

Defining Scientists

A scientist is someone who . . .

studies nature and the physical world by testing, experimenting, and measuring. (Scholastic, 1996)

Scientists . . .

try to find answers to questions they have about our world. Often, they improve our world by finding answers to their questions.

Handout 1A

Defining Scientists

A scientist is someone who . . .

studies nature and the physical world by testing, experimenting, and measuring.
(Scholastic, 1996)

Scientists . . .

try to find answers to questions they have about our world. Often, they improve our world by finding answers to their questions.

Handout 1A

Defining Scientists

A scientist is someone who . . .

studies nature and the physical world by testing, experimenting, and measuring.
(Scholastic, 1996)

Scientists . . .

try to find answers to questions they have about our world. Often, they improve our world by finding answers to their questions.

Handout 1B

What Scientists Do: The Wheel of Scientific Investigation and Reasoning

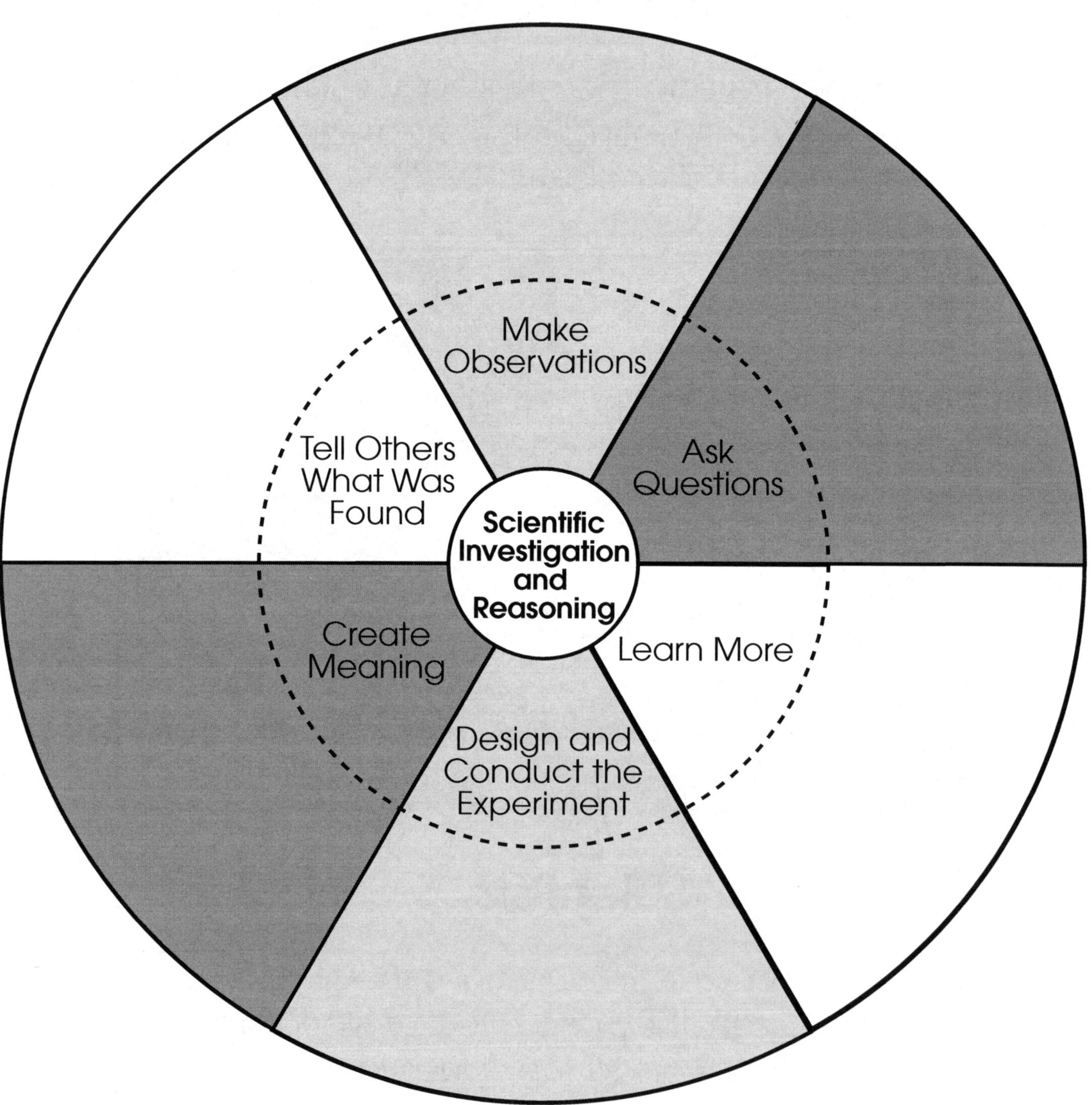

Lesson 2:
What Is a System?

Planning the Lesson

Instructional Purpose

- To review the concept preassessment with the class.
- To introduce the concept of systems.
- To apply understandings about systems to a new system.

Instructional Time

- 45 minutes

Systems Concept Generalizations

- Systems have parts (elements).
- Systems have boundaries.
- Systems have inputs and outputs.
- A system's elements interact with each other and a system's inputs.

Assessment "Look Fors"

- Students should be able to describe a system.

Materials/Resources/Equipment

- Chart paper
- Markers
- Slide of Handout 2A (Understanding Systems)
- Handouts of Handout 2B (System Definitions) and Handout 2C (Systems Diagram) for each student

Implementing the Lesson

> *Note to Teacher*: This lesson may be conducted whole class or in small groups of 2–4 students.

1. Distribute Handout 2A. Ask students to share their examples of systems from the preassessment activity. Write down all examples.
2. Now ask students to categorize their examples into what systems go together and why. Proceed until all systems have a category.
3. Now ask students: "What would be examples of things that are not systems?" (e.g., a broken-off limb from a tree, a withered leaf, or a stem)
4. Discuss generalizations about systems.
5. Distribute Handout 2B. Discuss system definitions.
6. Share the basic systems diagram model (Handout 2C) with the students and ask them to analyze their school as a system. Use the following questions:
   - What are the elements? (e.g., students, teachers, desks, books)
   - What are the boundaries? (e.g., school yard, building, property lines)
   - What are inputs? (e.g., rules from the School Board, parent and community ideas, state mandates)
   - What are outputs? (e.g., students who have learned important understandings)

- What are interactions *within* the system? (e.g., student-teacher, book-student, desk-student, teacher-teacher, student-student)
- What are interactions that are caused by inputs to the system? (e.g., district-school, school-state)
- Can you think of other examples of systems?

7. Discuss generalizations about systems, "What do all systems have?" Ask the group to look at the model of their school as a system. Which generalizations apply to all systems? (This may be done as a whole-group discussion or in small groups.)

Concluding and Extending the Lesson

Concluding Questions and/or Actions

- Generate and discuss ideas and share unit generalizations with the class. Indicate that they will be studying plants and seeing them as living systems in this unit of study.
- What new ideas about systems did you learn today?
- How can your generalizations about a school apply to other systems you know about?

What to Do at Home

- Ask students to discuss the school system with their parents. How does it work? How do the elements fit together? Students should come to the next class prepared to share additional ideas.

Name:______________________________ Date:__________

Handout 2A
Understanding Systems

Examples of Systems
Things That Are NOT Systems
Generalizations About Systems
• Systems have parts (elements). • Systems have boundaries. • Systems may have inputs and outputs. • A system's elements interact with each other and a system's inputs.

Handout 2B
System Definitions

1. *Element*—a distinct part of the system
2. *Boundary*—something that indicates or fixes a limit on the size or spread of a system
3. *Interaction*—the nature of connections made between/among elements and inputs of a system
4. *Input*—something that is put in the system
5. *Output*—something that is produced by the system; a product of the interactions

Systems Concept Generalizations

1. Systems have parts (elements).
2. Systems have boundaries.
3. Systems have inputs and outputs.
4. A system's elements interact with each other and a system's inputs.

Handout 2C
Systems Diagram

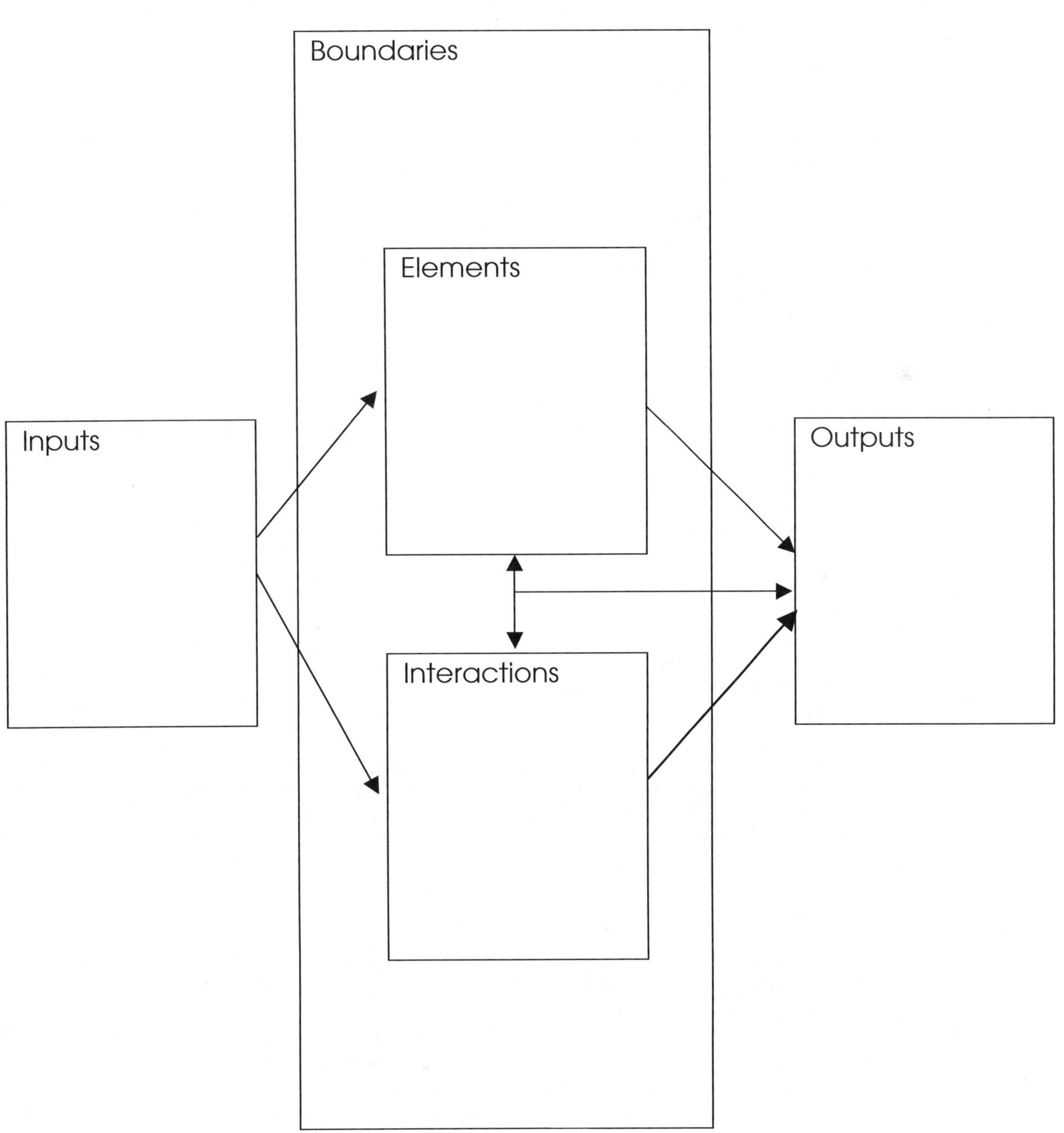

Lesson 3:
Terrariums as Systems

Planning the Lesson

Instructional Purpose

- To apply the concept of systems to a terrarium.
- To make generalizations about the terrarium as a system.

Instructional Time

- 45 minutes

Systems Concept Generalizations

- Systems have parts (elements).
- Systems have boundaries.
- Systems have inputs and outputs.
- A system's elements interact with each other and a system's inputs.

Key Science Concepts

- Plants have basic needs, including air, water, nutrients, and light.
- Plants are dependent on other living things and their surroundings for survival.
- Plants cause changes in the environment where they live.
- Plants produce oxygen and food.

Assessment "Look Fors"

- Students should be able to describe a terrarium as a system.

Materials/Resources/Equipment

- A large terrarium prepared according to Handout 3A (Making a Terrarium), *or* a terrarium purchased for use in the class
- Copies of Handout 3B (Terrarium)
- Chart paper
- Markers
- Sentence strips with the generalizations about systems
- Slides of Handouts 3A (Making a Terrarium), 3B (Terrarium), 3C (Completed Systems Model for a Terrarium), and 2B (System Definitions)
- Student log books

Implementing the Lesson

1. Tell students that they are going to be learning about plants during the *Budding Botanists* unit. Explain to students that they will be exploring the concept of systems while they work through this unit.
2. Divide students into small groups. Explain that a plant is an example of a system. Allow students to examine a terrarium. Ask students to look at Handout 3B of the terrarium. Have students discuss, draw, and label the parts of the terrarium. Use the following prompts for discussion:
   - What do you notice about the terrarium?
   - What things are part of the terrarium?

- What must go in?
- What comes out?

3. Have each group share what it included on its diagram. Begin grouping the ideas on a piece of chart paper to correspond with the categories of things in a system: elements, boundaries, inputs, outputs, and interactions (see Handout 3C for setup). Ask questions to enhance understanding and explain aspects of the system, including:
   - What are the parts of the terrarium (e.g., tank, soil, rocks, plants)?
   - What lives in a terrarium (e.g., plants, bacteria, insects)?
   - What other things have to be in the terrarium for the plants to live (e.g., water, food, carbon dioxide)? *Elements* are all of the things that are parts of the terrarium and what belongs in it.
   - What are the edges or boundaries of the system (e.g., the top of the tank, the glass boundary)? *Boundaries* help us understand where a system begins and what things are inside a system.
   - What things go into the terrarium from the outside (e.g., food, water, air, sunlight, plants, other objects)? What are some things that have to be added to the terrarium regularly to keep the plants alive (e.g., food, clean water, sunlight)? *Inputs* are the things that are put into a system to keep it going.
   - What things come out of the terrarium (e.g., water evaporates into the air, more plants may be produced and taken out for other terrariums, dead plants/leaves)? *Outputs* are the things that a system produces or lets out.
   - How do inputs interact with elements and produce outputs (e.g., the plants produce oxygen; the plants use sunlight to produce food)?
   - What do the plants do to use the inputs and give off outputs (e.g., photosynthesis, transpiration, reproduction)? *Interactions* are the things that happen in a system to use the inputs and give off the outputs in combination with elements. Tell students that there are many different kinds of systems. Some systems are small, and their boundaries, elements, inputs, outputs, and interactions are easy to see.

4. Share the system's definitions (Handout 2B) and show how they apply to the terrarium (Handout 3C). Review the following:
   - *element*–a distinct part of the system
   - *boundary*–something that indicates or fixes a limit on the size or spread of a system
   - *interaction*–the nature of connections made between/among elements and inputs of a system
   - *input*–something that is put in the system
   - *output*–something that is produced by the system; a product of the interactions

5. Write each of the generalizations about systems on a separate sentence strip to post in the classroom. Students will be using these generalizations in the upcoming lessons about plant systems.
   - Systems have parts (elements).
   - Systems have boundaries.
   - Systems have inputs and outputs.
   - A system's elements interact with each other and a system's inputs.

Concluding and Extending the Lesson

Concluding Questions and/or Actions

- Have students complete a log entry. Say, "In your log books, draw and label a terrarium with the inputs, outputs, elements, and boundaries."
- Students also can choose one of the generalizations about systems and write three or more sentences that explain how it applies to another system about which they know. Remind them to include their reasons or examples to show how the generalization is true. Then, they can draw their system example.

What to Do at Home

- Ask students to share the generalizations about systems with someone at home. They should ask a family member to give examples and nonexamples of systems, and explain why he or she made that determination.
- Ask students to identify examples of systems in their homes, then draw a diagram showing how the generalizations apply to this system.

Handout 3A
How to Make a Terrarium

Materials

- Any glass container that has a lid (suggested: 20-gallon aquarium)
- Activated charcoal (can be purchased at pet store)
- Bark-based potting soil
- Plants that have similar light and humidity requirements
- Premoistened sphagnum moss (can be purchased at any garden center or nursery)
- Distilled water

Directions (adapted from Holigan, n.d.):

1. Put a thick layer of activated charcoal into the glass container. It is used in a terrarium to drain the soil. The layer should be about 1–2 inches deep.
2. Pour in the potting soil. Bark-based potting soil absorbs water and doesn't dry out. There should be enough soil to cover the activated charcoal and provide a firm foundation for the plants.
3. Place the plants in the terrarium. Put the taller plants toward the back of the terrarium. Add more potting soil, enough to anchor the plants.
4. After all of the plants have been placed, add a little more potting soil to the terrarium. Spread it around evenly.

5. Add the premoistened sphagnum moss. Premoistened moss allows you to add moisture to the soil without making a mess. It also acts as decorative mulch for the plants.
6. Add distilled water. Tap water or well water contains chemicals that can build up in the terrarium over time, contaminating the pure environment. Start with just a little bit of water. Once the water is in, it's very difficult to remove. You can always add more later if you didn't put in enough to start.
7. Monitor your terrarium for the first few days. It will rain inside the terrarium every day, distributing the water throughout the environment. However, if you notice condensation on the inside of the container, it means that there is too much moisture. Simply remove the lid for a day or two to allow the extra moisture to evaporate, and then replace the lid.

Handout 3B

Terrarium

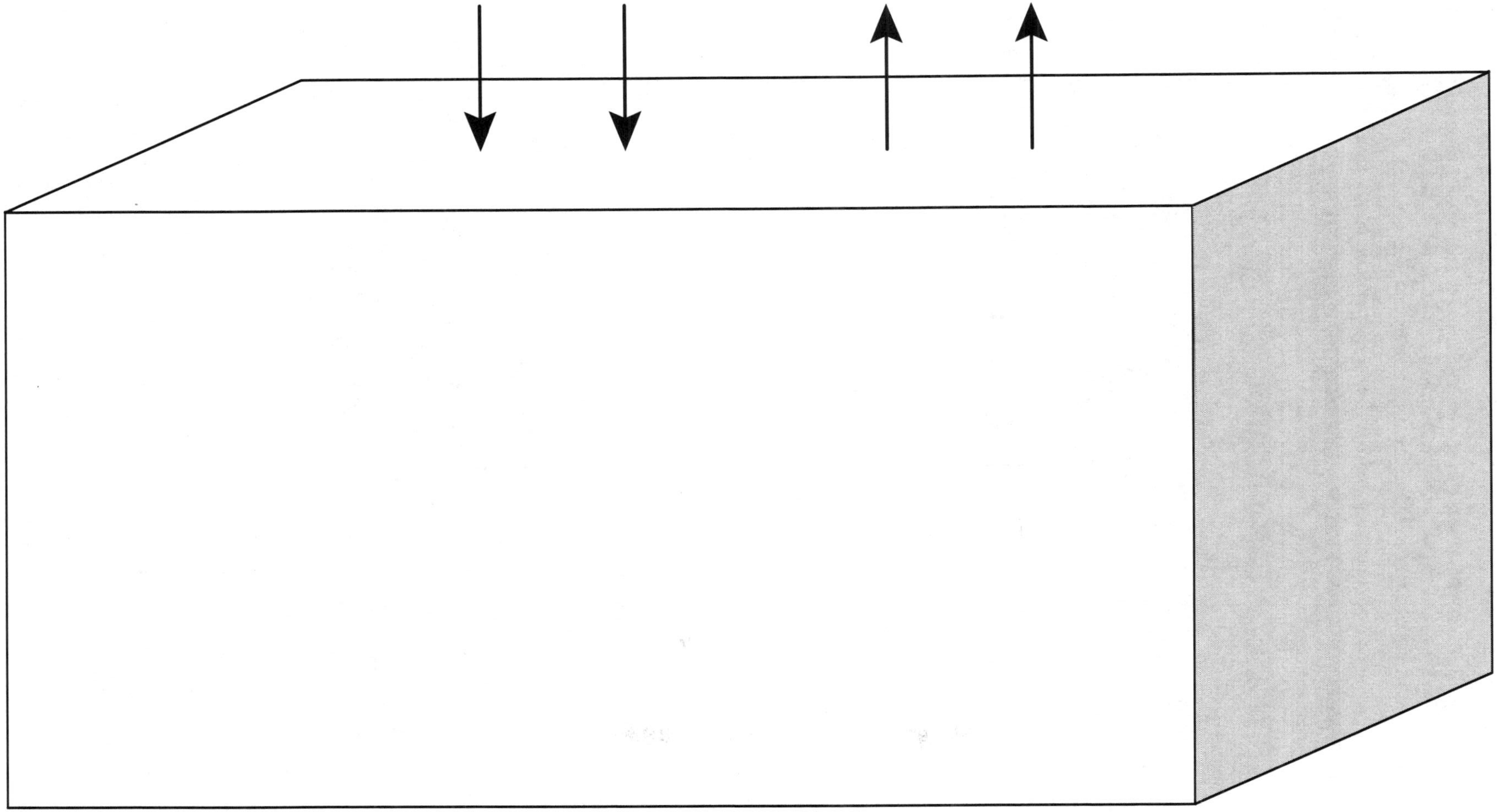

Handout 3C
Completed Systems Model for a Terrarium

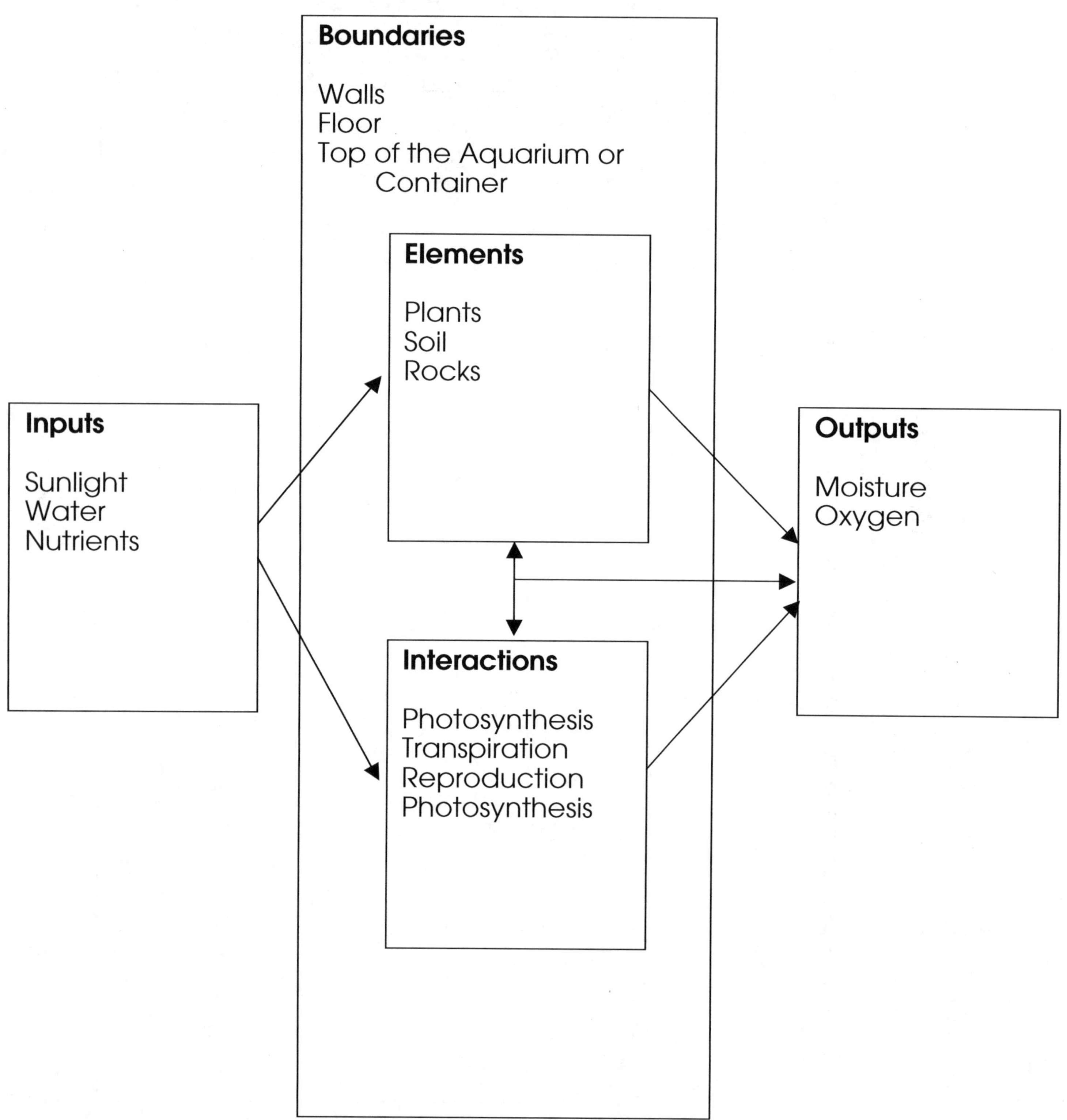

Lesson 4: What Scientists Do—Observe, Question, Learn More

Planning the Lesson

> **Note to Teacher**
> This two-part lesson is the first of two lessons developed to introduce scientific investigation and reasoning.
>
> For the next lesson you will need to soak 3–4 different kinds of seeds overnight (at least one of each kind of seed for each group of four students).

Instructional Purpose
- To introduce the Wheel of Scientific Investigation and Reasoning.
- To know how to conduct an experiment by making observations about flower petals.
- To observe seeds and how they change over time.

Instructional Time
- 60 minutes for Part I on Day 1
- 45 minutes for Part II on Day 2

Systems Concept Generalizations
- Systems have parts (elements).
- Systems have boundaries.

Key Science Concepts
- Plants have different parts that serve different functions in growth, survival, and reproduction.

Scientific Investigation Processes
- Make observations.
- Ask questions.
- Learn more.
- Design and conduct experiments.
- Create meaning.
- Tell others what was found.

Assessment "Look Fors"
- Students should be able to apply the steps of scientific investigation.
- Students should be able to interpret data from a data table.

Materials/Resources/Equipment
- Lab coat for teacher
- One lab coat (white adult T-shirt or dress shirt) for each student
- Charts or slides of Handouts 4A (Wheel of Scientific Investigation and Reasoning), 4B (Observations of Two Flowers), 4C (Steps for Flower Observation), 4D (Flower Observation Data Collection Table), and 4E (Seed Observations)
- Student copies or charts (if using small groups) of Handouts 4A, 4B, 4C, 4D, 4E
- Two kinds of flowers that have different petals in kind and number
- Markers or pens for students
- Sentence strip with the question "What are the parts of a seed?"

- Sentence strip with the question "Do all seeds have a seed coat?"
- Container with dried lima beans that have been soaked in water
- Container with dried lima beans
- Student log books
- Magnifying glasses

Implementing the Lesson

1. Have students put on lab coats. Explain to students that they are going to learn to "think like a scientist" and learn how to use the processes of science.
2. Distribute copies of the Wheel of Scientific Investigation and Reasoning (Handout 4A) to all students.
3. Discuss the six processes introduced on the wheel: (1) make observations, (2) ask questions, (3) learn more, (4) design and conduct experiments, (5) create meaning, and (6) tell others what was found. Tell students that scientists use these processes when learning about their world.
4. Using the wheel, prompt students to see the relationship between the scientific investigation processes and the wheel components. Have them draw or write their idea for each process to help them understand and remember. Prompt questions include:
   - What do you notice about the Wheel of Scientific Reasoning?
   - What processes do you think that scientists use *before* they conduct an experiment?
   - What do scientists do to conduct an experiment?
   - What do scientists do *after* they conduct an experiment?
   - Which part of an investigation do you think would be most difficult? Why?
   - Which order makes the most sense for these processes to progress?

5. Ask students to write and share their log responses to the prompt: "To think like a scientist means I will . . ."

Part I: Flower Observation

1. Explain to the class that they are going to use their senses to observe flowers. Divide the students into groups of 3–4 students and give each group two different kinds of flowers. Pick up one type of flower and ask each group to make observations of the flower and write the observations on the chart of Handout 4B. Questions to ask include:
   - What do you notice about the flower? What do you observe about the smell, the color, the petals, and the leaves?
   - When you make observations, you use your senses to learn. What sense do you use most to make observations?
   - What senses did you use to make these observations?

2. Ask each group to examine the second flower and make observations. Write the observations in the second column on the chart of Handout 4B.
3. Point to the "Ask Questions" section on the wheel. Have students think about questions they could ask when observing the two flowers. Ask students: "What questions do you have about flowers?" Write down the students' questions on chart paper.
4. Ask students to think about their flowers in a different way:

- How might you learn if one flower has more petals than another?
- How are the flower petals alike and how are they different?
- Why do you think that flowers have petals?

5. Point to the "Learn More" section of the wheel. Emphasize that the more students observe something, the more they can learn about it. Ask students what they noticed about the differences in the flowers. Pass out Handouts 4C and 4D. Ask students to follow the steps and record their observations about the number of petals.

Concluding and Extending the Lesson, Part I

Concluding Activity

- What were the results of the flower observation for each group?
- Why were group results different?
- What did you learn from doing this observation?

Concluding Questions

- If we think about a flower as a system, what role does the petal play in that system?
- Are your cut flowers a system? Why or why not?

What to Do at Home

- Ask students to observe other types of flowers they find in their yard or the neighborhood and share their observations of similarities and differences to the flowers observed in class.

Part II: Experiment With Seeds

1. Refer to the "Make Observations" section of the wheel. Point out concerns about using some senses for some investigations, such as why scientists wear goggles when doing experiments. Also, some things could be poisonous or harmful to the touch so you would not want to taste them or touch them. Explain that you know what the substance is so you are going to allow the students to use their senses to make observations. You should discuss the following with your students:
   - When might it be harmful to use some senses during an investigation?
   - How should you decide when it is not safe to use some senses during an investigation?
   - What are some ways that you can protect your senses during an investigation?

2. Create groups of 3–4 and assign roles for each group member. Review role responsibilities: recorder, reporter, supporter (manages materials, keeps the group on task, and encourages), and time keeper. Provide each group with one copy of Seed Observations (Handout 4E; *Note*: You may want to re-create the chart on chart paper to facilitate group use).
3. Show students lima beans that have *not* been soaked and then lima beans that *have* been soaked in water overnight. Give students magnifying glasses and allow them to observe the seeds closely. Explain that scientists sometimes use tables to record their observations. Ask the following:

- When you make observations, you use your senses to learn. What sense do you use most to make observations?
- Why would it be helpful for scientists to compare observations?
- How do scientists use observations to study systems?

4. Have the students work in their small groups for about 10 minutes and use Handout 4E to write down group observations according to sight, smell, and touch. Invite the reporters to share their findings with questions like:
   - What do you notice about our observations?
   - How are the two seeds alike? How are they different?

5. Direct students' attention to the second section on the wheel: "Ask Questions." Model this section by writing down one question you have on a sentence strip (do this ahead of time): "What are the parts of a seed?"
6. Ask students to tell you other questions they have about the seeds and write their questions on a large piece of chart paper. Guide the class to pick your question (or one similar to it) as the *one* question they want to answer.
7. Refer to the third step on the wheel: "Learn More." Ask students what can be done to learn more about something (e.g., Internet, books, experts), using the following prompts:
   - How can you learn more about something?
   - What do you think is the best way to learn? Why?

8. Point out that one way they can learn more is through additional observations. Demonstrate a seed dissection using a soaked lima bean. Show students the seed coat as you remove it from the seed. Ask students if they think all seeds have seed coats and show the sentence strip with the revised question. Say to students, "After learning more, I have a new question: Do all seeds have a seed coat?"
9. Tell students that they are going to complete the remaining steps on the Wheel of Scientific Investigation and Reasoning the next day: "Design and Conduct the Experiment," "Create Meaning," and "Tell Others What Was Found."
10. Soak several of three different kinds of seeds in water overnight (at least one of each kind of seed for each group of four students).
11. Pass out student log books and ask students to predict whether the seeds will have seed coats.

Concluding and Extending the Lesson, Part II

Concluding Questions and/or Actions

- Which of the systems generalizations do you think applied to our investigation of seeds?
- What do you think we will do tomorrow to conduct an experiment on our question?

What to Do at Home

- Ask students to work with a parent to set up and conduct simple experiments in their homes using the wheel.

Handout 4A

Wheel of Scientific Investigation and Reasoning

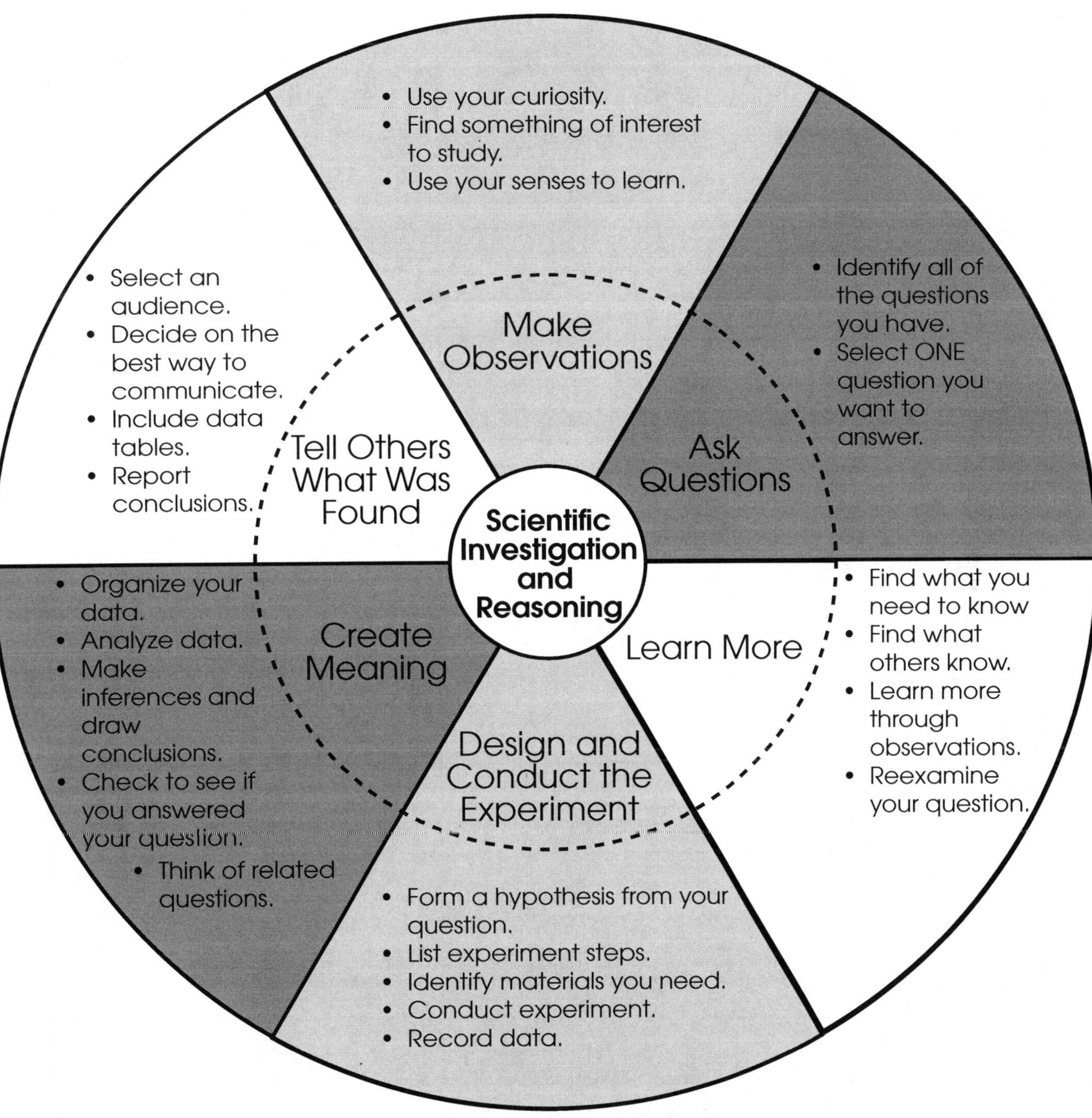

Note. Adapted from Kramer (1987).

Name:_______________________________ Date:____________

Handout 4B

Observations of Two Flowers

Sense	Flower #1	Flower #2
Smell		
Touch		
Sight		

Name:______________________________ Date:__________

Handout 4C

Steps for Flower Observation

1. Take one flower and count the number of petals on the flower.
2. Write the number in the correct space on the data table on the next page.
3. Take the second flower and count the number of petals on the flower.
4. Write the number of petals in the correct space on the data table.
5. Think about what the data table tells us.
6. Answer the question, "Did the two types of flowers have the same number of petals?"

Name:______________________________ Date:___________

Handout 4D

Flower Observation Data Collection Table

Question: Do the two types of flowers have the same number of petals?

Hypothesis: (What do you think?) We think the two types of flowers will have (circle one):

the same number of petals		a different number of petals

Data Table

Flower #1 Number of Petals	Flower#2 Number of Petals

Findings: (What did you find?) The flowers had (circle one):

the same number of petals		a different number of petals

Make Meaning: Our hypothesis is (circle one):

confirmed		refuted

Name:______________________________ Date:____________

Handout 4E

Seed Observations

Directions: Write your observations about your seeds below.

	Dried Seed	**Soaked Seed**
Appearance		
Feel		
Smell		

Lesson 5: What Scientists Do—Experiment, Create Meaning, Tell Others

Planning the Lesson

Instructional Purpose

- To continue using the Wheel of Scientific Investigation and Reasoning.
- To observe seeds and how they change over time.

Note to Teacher
This lesson is the second of two lessons developed to introduce scientific investigation and reasoning.

Instructional Time

- 45 minutes

Systems Concept Generalizations

- Systems have parts (elements).
- Systems have boundaries.
- Systems have inputs and outputs.
- A system's elements interact with each other and a system's inputs.

Key Science Concepts

- Plants have different parts that serve different functions in growth, survival, and reproduction.

Scientific Investigation Skills and Processes

- Make observations.
- Ask questions.
- Learn more.
- Design and conduct experiments.
- Create meaning.
- Tell others what was found.

Assessment "Look Fors"

- Students should be able to apply the steps of scientific investigation.
- Students should be able to interpret data from a data table.
- Students should be able to describe how the experiment was conducted and what results were found.

Materials/Resources/Equipment

- Lab coats for teacher and students
- Charts or slides of Handouts 4A (Wheel of Scientific Investigation and Reasoning), 5A (Definition of Hypothesis), 5B (Using a Question to Form a Hypothesis), 5C (Steps for Seed Experiment), 5D (Observations of Seeds), and 5E (Class Chart—Do All Seeds Have Seed Coats?)
- Student copies or charts of Handouts 5C and 5D
- Markers or pens for students
- Sentence strip with the question, "Do all seeds have a seed coat?"
- Three to four different kinds of seeds soaked overnight (at least one of each kind of seed for each group of four students)

- One badge per student using Handout 5F (Science Investigation Badges)
- Straightened paper clips
- Scissors
- Magnifying glasses
- Clear tape
- Chart paper
- Student log books

Implementing the Lesson

1. Put on lab coats and remind students of the problem they have been asked to solve: "Do all seeds have a seed coat?" Explain that it might be helpful to learn more about seeds.
2. Review what the class has done so far when investigating plants during the previous lesson (Lesson 4) and refer to the Wheel of Scientific Investigation and Reasoning (Handout 4A) when discussing the following:
   - What did we start investigating the other day?
   - How did we begin our investigation and what scientific processes did we apply?
   - What did we observe about the seed?
   - What question did we identify?

3. Move to the fourth process: "Design and Conduct the Experiment" on the Wheel (Handout 4A). Note that the first thing scientists do to conduct an experiment is to form a hypothesis from their question. Use Handout 5A to define hypothesis as "an educated guess or a prediction that can be tested about how a scientific investigation or experiment will turn out." Use Handout 5B to model your thinking process in turning your original question into a hypothesis.
4. Have students either turn to their partner or talk in small groups about other possible hypotheses that could come from the question and write down the hypotheses on chart paper. Discussion can include:
   - What other hypotheses could we form from the original question?
   - How did you come up with another hypothesis?

5. Explain that the hypothesis created by the students needs to be tested through an experiment. It is important to plan the experiment by listing the steps. Ask students to tell what they think needs to be done to conduct an experiment for the hypothesis. After students share, reveal the list of steps the class is going to follow (see Handout 5C). Point out the list of materials that are needed for the experiment.
6. Explain that scientists have to be careful about how they test a hypothesis or plan an experiment. They must think of all of the different things that could cause something to happen and then make sure that the experiment changes only one of those things. Identify the variables (e.g., type of seed, amount of time seeds were soaked, correct dissection of the seeds). Ask students: "Let's consider our experiment. What things could happen that might cause problems?"
7. Explain that scientists conduct each experiment more than once to make sure that what occurred isn't just a coincidence. The class is going to observe the teacher conduct the experiment once. The teacher will then conduct the experiment a second time with a few student assistants to illustrate group teamwork to the class. The third experiment will be conducted by students

without the teacher and will then be discussed by the whole class. (For many students, this may be their first exposure to conducting a scientific experiment; thus the students need to have it modeled for them.) Teachers should check the following:

- Does each group have the same seeds?
- Have all of the seeds been soaked the same amount of time?

8. Review how to dissect seeds and guide the group, step-by-step, to conduct the experiment at the same time. Ask each group to make observations and to write down what they observed on Handout 5D. Remind students of the question by asking, "Did each kind of seed have a seed coat?"
9. Tell students that they have just conducted a scientific investigation or experiment. They tested their hypothesis, and now they need to do the last two processes: "Create Meaning" from the data and "Tell Others What Was Found."
10. Explain that scientists use charts to organize their data so they can figure out or analyze what the data show—to *create meaning*. Ask the reporter from each group to share the group's findings. Use chart paper re-creating Handout 5E to record the findings. Tell students that they are to come up with an inference—a conclusion about whether the prediction or hypothesis was correct. Ask students:
    - Was there a seed coat on each kind of seed?
    - Was our hypothesis correct?
    - Did we answer our original question?
    - What other questions do you have?
    - What other experiments do you think we might do?

11. Explain that now the class needs to *tell others what was found*. Ask student pairs or small groups to decide who they should tell about their findings and how they should communicate their findings. Ask them, "What is important about what we found?"
12. Tell the student scientists they have just conducted a scientific investigation and give out "badges" saying "I Conducted an Experiment in Science—Ask Me About It" (Handout 5F). Also ask students to write the date in their log book and make one of the following entries in their student log books:
    - When it comes to conducting scientific investigations, the most difficult thing is . . .
    - The next investigation I would like to conduct on seeds is . . .

Concluding and Extending the Lesson

Concluding Questions and/or Actions

- Share student log book entries.
- What do you think we could have changed about the way we did the experiment?
- Which generalizations about systems did you observe in the experiment?

What to Do at Home

- Using their Wheel of Scientific Investigation and with an adult's help, ask students to conduct an experiment of their own about seeds. Remind them to write down the steps to the experiment.

Handout 5A

Definition of Hypothesis

A hypothesis is . . .

"an educated guess or prediction that can be tested about how a scientific investigation or experiment will turn out."

(Scholastic, 1996)

Handout 5B

Using a Question to Form a Hypothesis

My Question . . .

Do all seeds have the same seed parts?

I Learned More . . .

I dissected a lima bean that had been soaked in water and saw that the seed had an outer coating.

I Now Think . . .

I saw that the lima bean had a seed coating and changed my question. My new question to investigate is, "Do all seeds have a seed coat?

My Hypothesis . . .

All seeds have a seed coat.

Handout 5C

Steps for Seed Experiment

Hypothesis: All seeds have a seed coat.

Experiment Steps

1. Soak three to four different kinds of seeds in water overnight.
2. Take a seed out of the water and dissect it, checking to see if it has a seed coat. Use your magnifying glass to examine it closely.
3. Record your observations about the seed.
4. Take the second seed out of the water, dissect it, and use a magnifying glass to see if it has a seed coat.
5. Record your observations about the second seed.
6. Take the third seed out of the water, dissect it, and use a magnifying glass to look for the seed coat.
7. Record your observations about the third seed.

Materials Needed

- Three to four different kinds of seed soaked overnight
- scissors
- paper clip (opened)
- magnifying glass
- experiment data table

Handout 5D

Observations of Seeds

Group # ______________________________

Members ____________________ ____________________

____________________ ____________________

____________________ ____________________

____________________ ____________________

Type of Seed	Evidence of Seed Coat	Other Observations

Handout 5E

Class Chart—Do All Seeds Have Seed Coats?

Group	Seed #1	Seed #2	Seed # 3
Seed Type			
#1			
#2			
#3			
#4			
#5			
#6			

Conclusions and questions:

- ____
- ____
- ____
- ____
- ____
- ____
- ____
- ____

Handout 5F

Science Investigation Badges

I Conducted an Experiment in Science— Ask Me About It!

I Conducted an Experiment in Science— Ask Me About It!

I Conducted an Experiment in Science— Ask Me About It!

I Conducted an Experiment in Science— Ask Me About It!

I Conducted an Experiment in Science— Ask Me About It!

Lesson 6:
A Real-World Problem to Solve!

Planning the Lesson

Note to Teacher
This lesson begins a series of lessons throughout the rest of the unit where students are exposed to a scientist's log entries to accompany their understanding of plants. Small groups of students should form a team to discuss Professor Blackwell's notes as the lessons proceed. Resolutions to the problem of plants as a source of fuel for cars should be presented by these teams of students in Lesson 11.

Instructional Purpose

- To use the scientific process skills of observing, collecting data, and making inferences.
- To understand that locating resources is an important part of "learning more."

Instructional Time

- 45 minutes

Scientific Investigation Skills and Processes

- Make observations.
- Ask questions.
- Learn more.
- Create meaning.

Assessment "Look Fors"

- Students should be able to ask questions about the message and log entry.
- Students should be able to generate ideas for the Need to Know Board.

Materials/Resources/Equipment

- Pretaped phone message with situation from Handout 6A (Recording to Introduce the Scenario)
- Student log books
- Copies of Handout 6B (Professor Blackwell's Log Entry #1) for each student
- Slide or chart of Handout 6C (Need to Know Board)
- Pencils
- Markers

Implementing the Lesson

1. The teacher will introduce the unit scenario with a similar statement to the following: "You and your teammates have been called into action. Listen to the excited call that has come into central office and then grab your notebooks so you will be ready to begin! The message came from a dean at The College of William and Mary in Virginia" (see Handout 6A).
2. Allow students to listen to the phone message (prerecorded by teacher) for the team. Hand out and read aloud the first log entry from Professor Blackwell (Handout 6B). Hand out copies of the Need to Know Board (Handout 6C).
3. Guide students through the Need to Know Board using information from the tape and the copy of the first log entry. Have groups ask the following questions about the messages:
   - What do we know?

- What do we need to know?
- How can we find out?

4. Record student responses and ask students to decide how to proceed with the work in small investigatory teams of 4–5. Prompts to help with this decision include:
    - What should we do first? What next?
    - Who will investigate what questions?
    - What resources will we use?
    - What is our plan of action?

Concluding and Extending the Lesson

Log Prompt

- Students should answer the following in their log books:
    - o What would be the implications of finding a type of plant fuel? What groups would be affected? How? Why?

What to Do at Home

- Ask students to bring in a variety of plants from home to use in the classroom. These plants will be returned at the end of the unit.

Handout 6A

Recording to Introduce the Scenario

The following message was recorded and sent to the science team:

> We have been doing some building at the College and sent our staff to clean out some rooms in the science wing. In a closet filled with old boxes, we have found one of particular interest. In it were research logs from long ago. Many of them are old and very faded, but one of our graduate students thought it would be interesting to read them. What he discovered was amazing! Despite the bad condition the science lab logs were in and the fact that there are many pages of data missing, a researcher seems to be saying he had found a plant that could be used to fuel cars! Can you imagine? What would that mean to the world? Naturally, we thought of your team immediately. If anyone can help us piece together the research and understand the experiments that this scientist could have done, it would have to be you. Needless to say, you can have complete access to all our facilities. However, we need you to work quickly and complete the work over the next 6 weeks, as after that time the College will be closed for construction, making the labs inaccessible.

Handout 6B
Professor Blackwell's Log Entry #1

I have secured enough grant money to begin my research. My family thinks I have completely lost my mind. I am determined that science has progressed so far that we can indeed find the way to use plants for anything if we have the patience to look and experiment. It is still my belief that somewhere on this planet I will be able to find ways to use plants to fuel cars!

My associates keep asking me if I truly intend to travel to all parts of the world to find out about different fuels and different uses for plants other than eating or medicine.

Perhaps I never will find the solution, but to me it seems a worthwhile venture. I will keep my personal log up to date throughout the trip as it helps me to reflect and keep focused. Of course, we will carry some equipment, but much of the research will be done here at our laboratories once we have taken specimens and interviewed the peoples of the lands we explore. What a grand adventure we are about to embark on! It is with some fear but much excitement that I begin this research.

Name:_______________________________ Date:_______________

Handout 6C

Need to Know Board

What Do We Know? **What Do We Need to Know?** **How Can We Find Out?**

What Have We Learned?

Lesson 7: Animal, Vegetable, or Mineral: What Is It?

Planning the Lesson

Instructional Purpose

- To understand the distinguishing characteristics and qualities of plants.

Instructional Time

- 45 minutes

Systems Concept Generalizations

- Systems have parts (elements).
- Systems have boundaries.
- Systems have inputs and outputs.
- A system's elements interact with each other and a system's inputs.

Key Science Concepts

- Plants have basic needs, including air, water, nutrients, and light.
- Plants have different parts that serve different functions in growth, survival, and reproduction.
- Different plants have different characteristics.

Scientific Investigation Skills and Processes

- Make observations.
- Learn more.
- Create meaning.

Note to Teacher

If not done earlier, classrooms should have a Research Learning Center set up where students can find books, magazines, pictures, encyclopedias, etc., on the topic of plants. Teachers may include seed catalogues, picture books, fiction, and nonfiction books. They also may want to include field guides to trees, flowers, and plants. Lesson 9 requires sprouted bean plants. Plant seeds at least 2 weeks before you will need the plants. You will need about three for each student. To allow for some plants to die, you may want to sprout at least three times as many seeds as you will actually need.

Assessment "Look Fors"

- Students should be able to use correct definitions for plants.
- Students should be able to apply the generalizations about systems to a plant.

Materials/Resources/Equipment

- Student log books
- Research Learning Center (see Note to Teacher)
- A number of healthy potted plants for observation
- Magnifying glasses
- Chart paper
- Markers
- Copies of Handout 7A (Definition of a Plant, Part I) and Handout 7B (Definition of a Plant, Part II) for each student
- Slides of Handout 7C (Professor Blackwell's Log Entry #2) and Handout 7D (The Elements of a Plant System)
- Slide and handouts of Handout 7E (Concept Map of a Plant)

Implementing the Lesson

1. Put several plants around the room on tables/desks for students to observe. Give students magnifying glasses to use as they observe the plants. (Teachers may want to take a few minutes to allow students to retrieve selected books on the subject of plants to be used at their desks or in their groups.)
2. Read Professor Blackwell's Log Entry #2 to the students (Handout 7C). Remark to students that scientists often need to create categories to help them organize ideas. For living things, two of the categories we know best are plants and animals. Write the word *plant* on the board. Ask students how they would explain the difference between plants and animals. Tell students that they are going to use their skills of observation to construct a definition of a plant. Give students Handout 7A (Definition of a Plant, Part I). Direct students to draw a plant in the appropriate box, then use the graphic organizer to collect their ideas about plants.
3. Give students Handout 7B (Definition of a Plant, Part II). Have students brainstorm in pairs the definition and description of a plant. Each student should complete the top half of Handout 7B. Ask students to give examples and nonexamples of plants. Discuss the definitions the students have constructed and create a consensus definition of a plant that students will copy onto the lower half of Handout 7B.
4. Now ask students to describe a plant as a system: What are its elements, its boundaries, its inputs and outputs, and its interactions?
5. Pass out Handout 7D to review plant elements. Fully describe the plant elements. Ask students to draw in inputs and outputs. Discuss what a boundary might be for plants.
6. Tell students they will be studying various plant interactions in upcoming lessons.

Concluding and Extending the Lesson

Concept Mapping Practice

- Lead students in creating a concept map on plants. Please see "Concept Mapping" in Appendix B as a guide for instructing students in concept mapping. To begin this activity, tell students: "We have conducted experiments on flowers and seeds in order to understand plants better. Let's review what we now understand about plants. I am going to teach you how you can show what you have learned and understand in a way that will help you remember." Show them the slide of Handout 7E and distribute copies of Handout 7E. Use the following questions as a guide for completing the concept map activity.
  - What are the parts of plants?
  - What do plants require to grow?
  - What is the relationship of a seed to a plant?

Log Prompt

- Describe how a plant is a system. How are plants different from animals as living things and systems? What do you think?

Concept Mapping

- Have students create their own concept maps about other plant elements.

What to Do at Home

- Students should pick out a plant at home to study. Using their understanding of plants, students should analyze it as a system. How is it unique from other plants? If possible, students should bring in the plant and the drawing of its features to share orally with the class.

Name:______________________________ Date:____________

Handout 7A

Definition of a Plant, Part I

Directions: Draw a picture of a plant in the box below and label its parts.

Name:______________________________ Date:____________

Handout 7B

Definition of a Plant, Part II

My Definition of a Plant

A plant is:

____

____

____

____

Examples	Nonexamples

Our Class Definition of a Plant

A plant is:

____

____

____

____

Handout 7C

Professor Blackwell's Log Entry #2

We have already covered so much territory and so many countries. I now have some very promising information. In our interviews at this location we have found that the people are using plants in many different ways. Could it be we have found a spot in the world where people have found plants a good source of energy? If so, it warrants greater research and resources. The people that live here are unable to read or write, but they have been a great source of help. It took a bit of explaining to get my needs across to them. When I asked the people for the different kinds of plants they use for energy, they looked confused and instead began to tell me about their animals. I haven't given any thought to what the difference is between an animal and plant since I was in elementary school. Perhaps it would do me good to give a quick class to my "team" on what I am looking for in detail. What makes a plant a plant? I hate to waste time and resources by having to explain to each one when they bring in things like rocks or small animals.

Handout 7D

The Elements of a Plant System

The Parts of a Plant

Flowers are part of the plant that lets plants reproduce. Flowers make seeds and seeds grow into new plants.

Leaves are important. Leaves have chlorophyll. Leaves use chlorophyll to make food for the plant.

The stem works like a straw. The stem takes water from the roots to other parts of the plant. The stem takes food made by the leaves to other parts of the plant.

The roots hold the plant in the soil. The roots take in water from the soil for the plant to use.

Name:______________________________ Date:____________

Handout 7E

Concept Map of a Plant

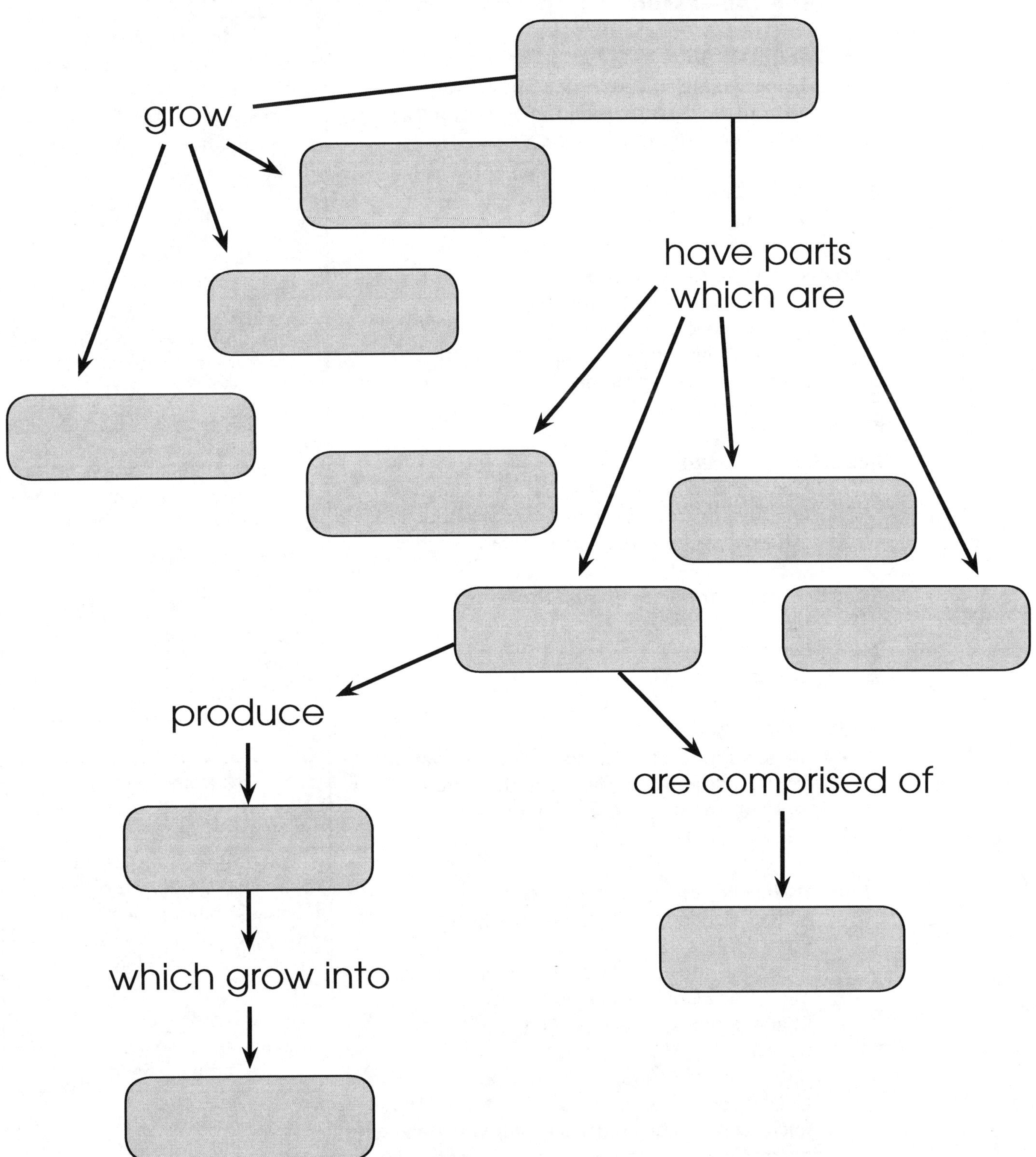

Lesson 8:
Close Up: Using a Microscope

Planning the Lesson

Instructional Purpose

- To investigate and understand basic plant anatomy, including the nature of plant cells, through use of a microscope.

Instructional Time

- 45 minutes

Systems Concept Generalizations

- Systems have parts (elements).
- Systems have boundaries.
- Systems have inputs and outputs.
- A system's elements interact with each other and a system's inputs.

Key Science Concepts

- Plants have different parts that serve different functions in growth, survival, and reproduction.
- Different plants have different characteristics.

Scientific Investigation Skills and Processes

- Make observations.
- Learn more.
- Create meaning.

Assessment "Look Fors"

- Students should be able to record observations from a slide and apply labels appropriately.
- Students should be able to handle the microscopes correctly.

Materials/Resources/Equipment

- Slide of Handout 8A (Professor Blackwell's Log Entry #3)
- Slides and copies of Handouts 8B (What I Saw: Microscope Observation Worksheet)
- Charts or slides of Handout 6C (Need to Know Board)
- Microscopes (preferably one for every two to three students; teachers may want to set up the microscopes to be used in step 6 before beginning class)
- Microscope slides to view (a boxed set of plant slides)

Note to Teacher

More than one microscope may be brought into the classroom. If possible, a dissecting scope should be made available. Students should become familiar with more than one type of microscope.

Make sure students understand that there are two lenses: the ocular and the objective. To get the total magnification, one must multiply the powers of the two lenses together. The ocular is always 10x. Students can be taught to just add a zero to the end of the number on the objective (multiply by 10) to get the total magnification.

A computer microscope can be used in the classroom if one is available. Students should become familiar with use and preparation of technology-based viewing.

Note to Teacher

For the next lesson, soak lima beans in water overnight. Lesson 10 requires sprouted bean plants. Plant seeds at least 2 weeks before you will need the plants. You will need about three for each student. To allow for some plants to die, you may want to sprout at least three times as many seeds as you will actually need.

Implementing the Lesson

1. Explain to the team that you have received a new package with information. Read Professor Blackwell's Log Entry #3 (Handout 8A). Show students a box of prepared slides to represent the slides mentioned in the log entry.
2. Return to the Need to Know Board from Lesson 6 (Handout 6C). Ask students:
   - What new information should be added to the board?
   - What new questions do you have?
   - What skills do you need to proceed further with the investigation?

3. Introduce the microscope: Explain to students that in scientific work the use of a microscope helps the biologist see things that are beyond what we can see with just our eyes. Explain that the microscope is an important tool, but also a very delicate one that needs to be cared for properly. *In order to be allowed to use the microscope, students will need to prove they can use the microscope properly.*
4. Show students how to carry the microscope using the neck or arm and holding carefully onto the base at the same time, if it is to be moved at all. Demonstrate to students how to lower the platforms as far down as possible. Show how to secure the slide on the stage and place the image in the center of the field. Once it is centered, make sure the microscope is set on the lowest setting and adjust the height until the image is within field. Once it is centered and in view, move it to a higher setting and focus.
5. Show students how to draw what they have seen on the sheets for observation and record necessary data such as specimen name and date. Make sure that students understand that only what they see through the microscope lens is drawn inside the circles. All other writing and drawing is done outside the circle.
6. Place a slide on the microscope, focus it, and then have each student look at the slide and record what he or she sees.
7. When the teacher is satisfied that students are ready to use the microscopes independently, they will observe three or more slides and then draw their observations on the What I Saw: Microscope Observation Worksheet (Handout 8B). After all students have completed the assignment, discuss what they saw and how they labeled their drawings.

Concluding and Extending the Lesson

Discussion Questions

- What observations did you make about specific elements of the special plant?
- What might this mean? Can you hypothesize?

Log Prompt

- What new ideas did you have about plants as a result of seeing them "close up"?

What to Do at Home

- Students should observe a plant in their garden or a neighbor's garden, then talk with an adult about differences among garden plants.

Handout 8A

Professor Blackwell's Log Entry #3

I am so glad to be home. I am in my laboratory. The new microscopes are here. I have discovered an interesting thing about the plants from the island. The cells of one special plant are different. I have never seen a plant cell like it. We have brought plant slides from the island. I want to confirm my hypothesis. I must be careful that I am not letting my imagination get the better of me.

Name:______________________________ Date:____________

Handout 8B

What I Saw: Microscope Observation Worksheet

Slide #1: ____

Magnification __________

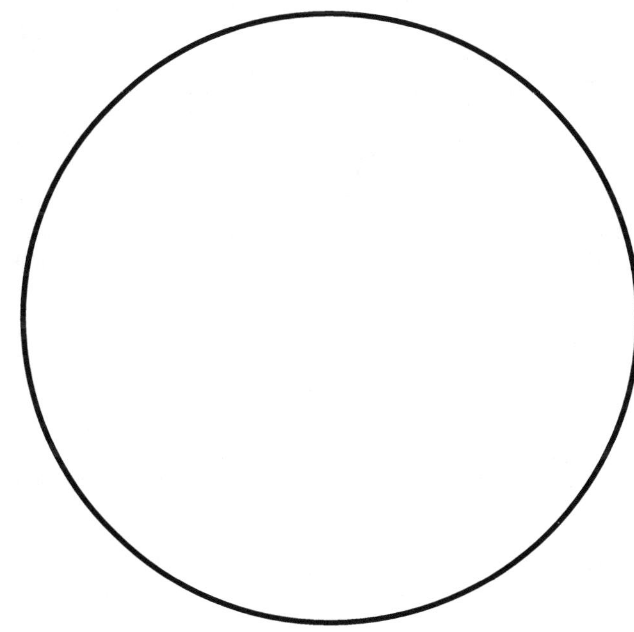

Slide #2: ____

Magnification __________

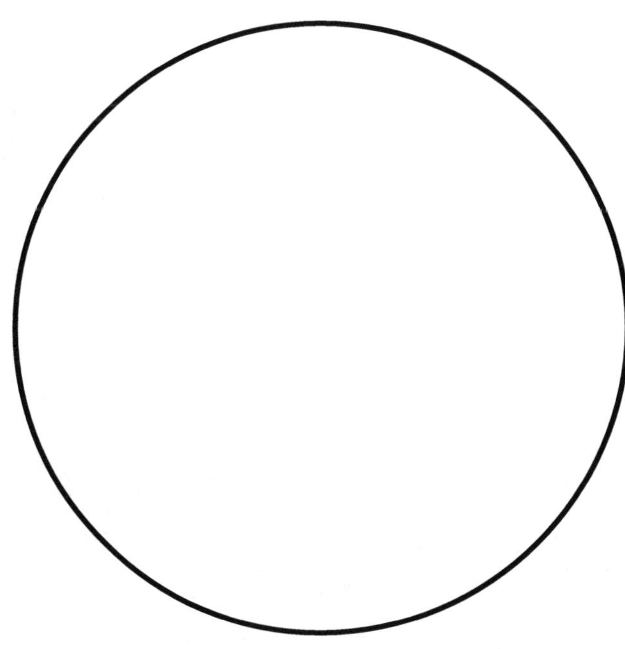

Slide #3: ____

Magnification __________

Slide #4: ____

Magnification __________

Lesson 9:
Just a Little Seed

Planning the Lesson

> **Note to Teacher**
> This lesson begins a seed observation study for the students. Results should be shared in the lesson on independent and small-group investigations.

Instructional Purpose

- To create a mini greenhouse using zipper bags and seeds to germinate seeds.
- To observe and document seed development and growth.
- To dissect seeds and identify seed parts.

Instructional Time

- 45 minutes

Systems Concept Generalization

- Systems have parts (elements).
- Systems have boundaries.
- Systems have inputs and outputs.
- A system's elements interact with each other and a system's inputs.

Key Science Concepts

- Plants have different parts that serve different functions in growth, survival, and reproduction.
- Plants undergo many changes during their life cycles.

Scientific Investigation Skills and Processes

- Make observations.
- Ask questions.
- Learn more.
- Design and conduct experiments.
- Create meaning.
- Tell others what was found.

Assessment "Look Fors"

- Students should be able to look at a dissected seed, point to the parts of the seed, name the parts, and explain the function.

Materials/Resources/Equipment

- Slides and copies of Handout 9A (How to Make Your Own Greenhouse), Handout 9B (Experimental Report Form), and Handout 9C (Parts of a Seed)
- Plastic zipper bags
- Computers (optional)
- Student log books
- Paper towels
- Water
- Lima bean seeds (enough for each student to have six to eight) that have been soaked in water overnight
- Straightened paper clips (for dissecting)

- Scissors (for dissecting)
- Slide of Handout 9D (Professor Blackwell's Log Entry #4)

Implementing the Lesson

1. Give students Handouts 9A, 9B, and 9C for the lesson. Review the Wheel of Scientific Investigation and Reasoning with students. Explain that the two investigations they are going to do will give them insight into the sprouting seed activity.
2. Have students observe the seeds that you brought in for this project and ask them what they are observing. Model for students how to create their "greenhouses" using Handout 9A as a guide.
   - Each greenhouse needs one zipper bag, a damp paper towel, and three or four seeds.
   - Fold the paper towel so it will fit into the bag and lay flat.
   - Move up from the bottom of the bag about 1 ½ inches and staple the bag, creating a barrier, so when seeds are inserted they do not fall completely to the bottom. This allows the roots to grow down.

3. Have students label the zipper bags with their names using a waterproof marker. Students will create their own bags in which they will germinate different seeds. They will place seeds in the bag and zip the bag closed. They should place their "greenhouses" near a window where they will receive sunlight. Students will observe their greenhouses every day and write their observations in their notebooks. This observation will be ongoing for several days, depending on how much you want the students to observe.
4. After completing the greenhouse, students will record their ongoing investigation process using Handout 9B.
5. Students will create a data table to organize data and information as they record their observations. Data sheets and graphs should be put in the students' notebooks. They may create them with paper and pencil or use a computer program.
6. After students have prepared their "greenhouses," provide each student with two or more lima beans, scissors, and straightened paper clips for dissecting the seeds. (Lima bean seeds should be soaked in water for 24 hours to make the dissection easier.)
7. Review that seeds have several different parts. Remind students of the investigation done earlier in the unit to discover whether seeds have seed coats. Questions to ask include:
   - Do you think seeds have other different parts too?
   - How could we find out?
   - If we dissect a seed, what do you think we will find?
   - What leads you to think that?

8. Direct students to the handout of seed parts (Handout 9C), then review the following:
   - seed coat (the outer covering),
   - the cotyledon (the fleshy part that provides nutrients to the plant as it develops inside the seed),
   - the first leaves, and
   - the primary root.

Ask students to carefully dissect their seeds and identify the parts in their seeds. Students will compare the germination of their bean seeds with the other seeds they are dissecting.

9. Explain to students that in order to continue to learn about seeds and plants they will begin working on a project.
10. Show Handout 9D from Professor Blackwell.

Concluding and Extending the Lesson

Discussion Questions

- What seed parts were you able to find?
- How can we find out the function of each of the parts of the seed?
- How do our generalizations about systems apply to seeds?

Log Prompt

- Describe how a greenhouse is an example of a system.
- How do you think a seed from a desert plant would be different in development inside the greenhouse from a lima bean seed?

What to Do at Home

- Have students assemble their own seed collections, identifying the plants the seeds have come from. They should include at least 10 examples of seeds, label them neatly, and provide information about each. Students will present their collections to the class at the end of the unit.

Handout 9A
How to Make Your Own Greenhouse

1. Collect your materials. You need one zipper bag, a damp paper towel, and three or four seeds.
2. Fold the paper towel so it will fit into the bag and lay flat.
3. Move up from the bottom of the bag about 1 ½ inches and staple the bag all the way across, creating a barrier, so when the seeds are inserted they do not fall completely to the bottom. This allows the roots to grow down.
4. Label the zipper bag with your name using a waterproof marker.
5. Place your greenhouse near a window where it will receive sunlight.

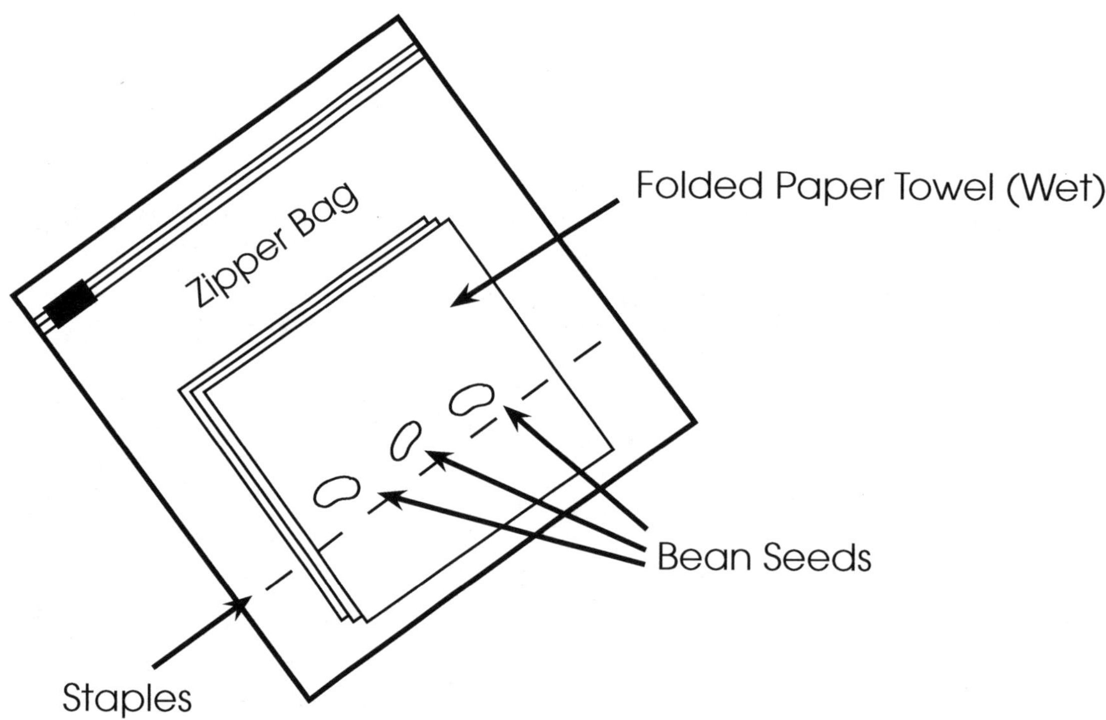

Note. Adapted from Ortiz and Kazilek (2003)

Name:______________________________ Date:____________

Handout 9B

Experimental Report Form

Name of Experiment: ______________________________

1. What was your hypothesis (or prediction about what would happen)?

____

____

____

____

2. What materials did you use to test the hypothesis?

____

____

____

____

3. What methods did you use? (Outline your steps below.)

- ______________________________
- ______________________________
- ______________________________
- ______________________________
- ______________________________
- ______________________________
- ______________________________

4. What data have been collected? Where are your data recorded? (Attach your data table to this sheet.)

____

____

____

____

5. What are your findings? (Did your hypothesis prove to be true or false?)

____

____

____

____

6. What new questions do you have?

____

____

____

____

Handout 9C
Parts of a Seed

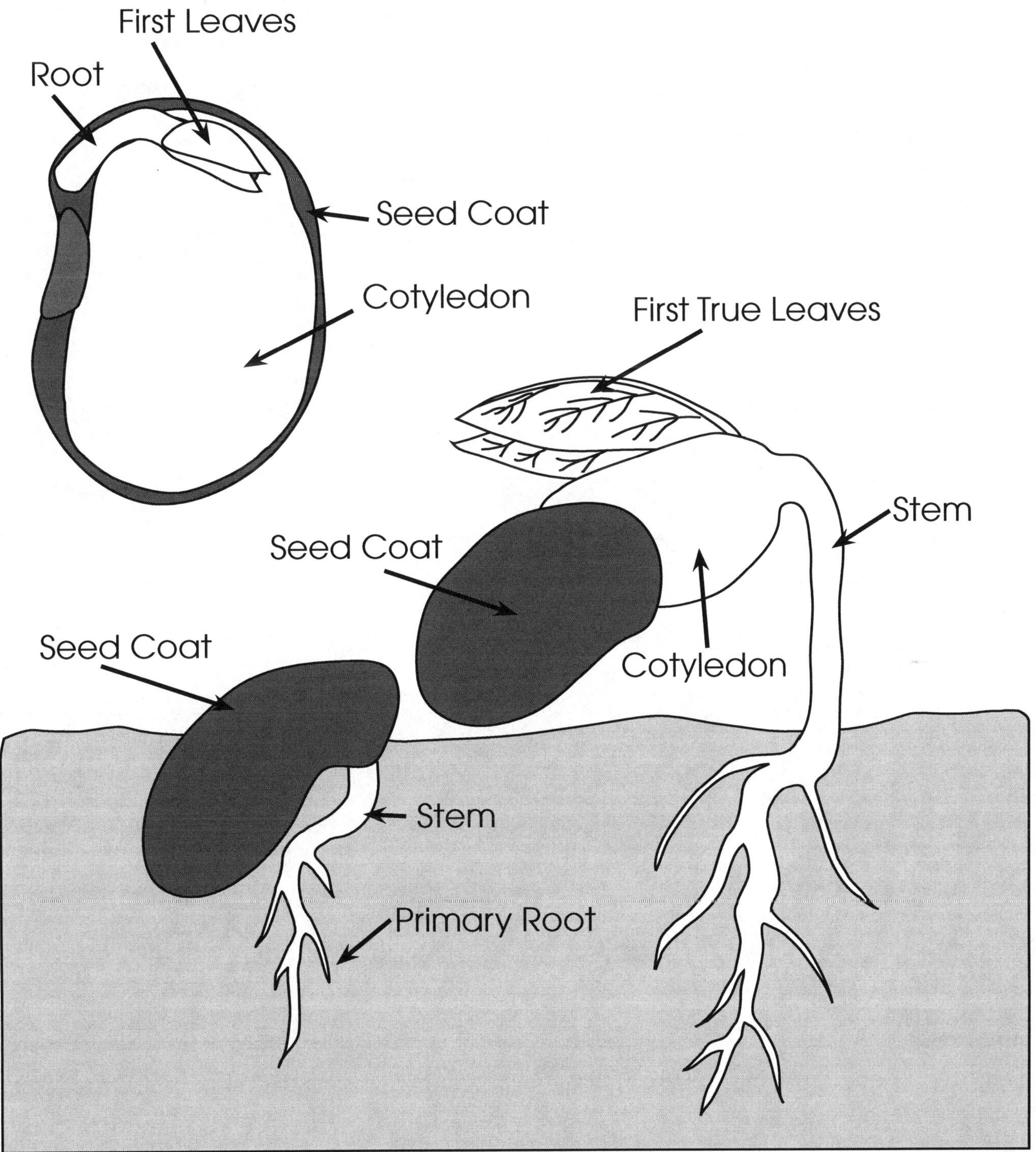

Handout 9D

Professor Blackwell's Log Entry #4

Once I have seen the seedlings and adult seeds and know what the plant is like, I will be able to begin the search for a way to reproduce these plants in large numbers. I cannot wait to get back home to my lab to continue this research for the plant fuel!

Lesson 10: Plant Experimentation on Basic Needs

Planning the Lesson

Note to Teacher
Fill out a class chart similar to Handout 10C on which each group is identified and its variables are noted.

Instructional Purpose

- To investigate and understand basic plant life processes.
- To demonstrate an understanding of plant system interactions.

Instructional Time

- 45 minutes for the initial lesson
- 5–10 minutes daily for ongoing observations over 2 weeks

Systems Concept Generalizations

- Systems have parts (elements).
- Systems have boundaries.
- Systems have inputs and outputs.
- A system's elements interact with each other and a system's inputs.

Key Science Concepts

- Plants have basic needs, including air, water, nutrients, and light.
- Plants are dependent on other living things and their surroundings for survival.
- Plants have different parts that serve different functions in growth, survival, and reproduction.
- Plants undergo many changes during their life cycles.

Scientific Investigation Skills and Processes

- Make observations.
- Ask questions.
- Learn more.
- Design and conduct experiments.
- Create meaning.
- Tell others what was found.

Assessment "Look Fors"

- Students should be able to record a hypothesis or prediction.
- Students should be able to identify materials used to test a hypothesis.
- Students should be able to outline and follow steps to test the hypothesis.
- Students should be able to make observations and record data.
- Students should be able to determine whether the hypothesis was proven and describe the findings.
- Students should be able to identify new questions.

Materials/Resources/Equipment

- Student log books
- Chart or slide of Handout 4A (Wheel of Scientific Investigation and Reasoning)

- Slide of Handout 10A (Professor Blackwell's Log Entry #5)
- Slides and copies of Handout 9B (Experimental Report Form) and Handout 10B (Examining Features of Experiments)
- Slide or copies of Handout 10C (Model for a Data Table)
- Computers (optional)
- Cameras (optional)
- Bean seeds from Lesson 9 that have sprouted into small plants (You will need about three for each student. To allow for some plants to die, you may want to sprout at least three times as many seeds as you will actually need.)
- Potting soil
- Playground sand
- Containers for planting seedlings (three for each student or three per group of students—you can use small plastic cups)

Implementing the Lesson

Note to Teacher
Please review the content notes on photosynthesis, respiration, and transpiration (pp. 10–11) before teaching this lesson.

1. Review the Wheel of Scientific Investigation and Reasoning (Handout 4A) with the students. Tell students that they are going to investigate the question, "What do plants need to survive?" Present the question by writing it on the board or overhead. Ask students to state their hypotheses about what plants need. Lead students to hypothesize that plants need light, water, soil, and food to grow. If students have another prediction that is feasible to test, add another "need" and another experimental group. Have students state these as hypotheses: "I think plants need . . . (water, soil, food/nutrients, light)." Ask students how they could test each hypothesis.
2. Discuss the roles of scientists as they conduct an experiment. Read Professor Blackwell's Log Entry #5 (Handout 10A). What are his concerns?
3. Create groups of 2–3 students. Depending on class size, several groups will be assigned to each experiment: light, soil, water, and nutrients. Assign groups. Give students Handout 10B (Examining Features of Experiments). Remind students that when doing an experiment it is important to control all of the variables that are not being tested. Have each group identify which components they will control.

Planning the Experiments

1. Present students with Handout 9B (Experimental Report Form). Assign one hypothesis to each group:
    - I think a plant needs light to survive.
    - I think a plant needs water to survive.
    - I think a plant needs food/nutrients to survive.
    - I think a plant needs soil to survive.

2. Challenge each group to complete Handout 9B to plan an experiment that will test the hypothesis they were assigned. As groups work, circulate among them to assist students in planning their experiments. Groups should plan experiments similar to those on the next page: (Teachers may want to give students the following procedures written on index cards if students are unable to generate them independently.)

FOR LIGHT:

1. Label the plants A, B, and C.
2. All three plants should be planted in the same kind of soil.
3. Plant A will be covered with a brown paper bag and placed in a dark place (closet) in the classroom.
4. Plant B will be placed in the classroom near the window.
5. Plant C will be placed in a dark corner of the room, under a table, or in another place where it will receive limited light.
6. Check and record findings for all three plants on a daily basis, watering the plants as necessary.

FOR SOIL:

1. Label plants A, B, and C.
2. Each plant will be planted in a different soil.
3. A will be planted in sand.
4. B will be planted in potting soil.
5. C will be planted in a half-and-half mixture of sand and potting soil.
6. All three plants will be located in the same general area near a window where they will receive sunlight.
7. Check and record findings for all three plants on a daily basis, watering the plants as necessary.

FOR WATER:

1. Label plants A, B, and C.
2. All three plants should be planted in the same kind of soil and placed in the same general area near a classroom window where they will receive sunlight.
3. Each plant will be given a different treatment.
4. Plant A will be watered when needed.
5. Plant B will be watered every day and kept wet.
6. Plant C will be watered only on Day 1 of the experiment.
7. Check and record findings for all three plants on a daily basis.

FOR FOOD/NUTRIENTS:

1. Label plants A, B, and C.
2. Each plant will be planted in the same soil and placed in the same general area near a window where it will receive sunlight.
3. Each plant will be given a different solution of nutrients.
4. Label gallon containers Solution #1, Solution #2, and Solution #3.
5. Fill Solution #1 container with clean, clear water.
6. Fill Solution #2 container with clean water and fertilizer.
7. Fill Solution #3 container with clean water mixed with 1 cup of detergent.
8. Plant A will be watered with Solution #1 (clear water).
9. Plant B will be watered with Solution #2 (water containing fertilizer).
10. Plant C will be watered with Solution #3 (water containing a pollutant such as detergent).
11. Use a measuring device (e.g., cup, beaker, graduated cylinder) to make sure that each time plants are watered, they all receive the same amount of water.
12. Check and record findings for all three plants on a daily basis, watering the plants as necessary.

3. Student groups will set up the four experiments to show how plants react to having one of their life needs unmet. This activity will be ongoing for 2 weeks. Students will record their findings on a daily or semidaily basis using copies of Handout 9B (Experimental Report Form). Extra copies of Handout 9B should be made available for students as they need them. In each experiment, students may use only one plant for each part of the experiment (A, B, C) or they may want to increase the experiment's reliability by having each student choose a plant for A, B, and C. This would provide several plants for each experiment. Have students begin filling out Handout 10B with a description of the plants when they begin the experiments.
4. Students will need to create data tables. They should be created on computers, if possible, and data entered as the experiments continue. If computers are not available, students may create their own data tables (see Handout 10C). Students will record plant observations on a semidaily basis for 2 weeks (i.e., count the leaves, measure the height, note the color of the plants, etc.).

Concluding and Extending the Lesson

Discussion Questions

- Why is regular observation important in experimentation?
- How do plants change over time? Why?
- How do plants change under different conditions? Why?

Log Prompts

- Describe how conducting an experiment is like a system.
- What aspects of designing and doing an experiment are easy for me? Which ones are difficult? Why?

What to Do at Home

- Ask students to design a plant experiment of their own, using the Experimental Report Form as a guide. Have them bring their design to class.

Handout 10A

Professor Blackwell's Log Entry #5

I have begun to understand that this plant is very important. We need to know how it will grow best in our laboratory. Our water here is like the water on the island. I need to find out how much water it needs. How much light does it need? What kind of soil does it need? To grow strong and healthy plants, I need the kind of soil the plant likes best. I must meet the needs of the plant. It would be a disaster if I killed the seedlings and could not find more plants in the wild!

Name:______________________________ Date:_______________

Handout 10B

Examining Features of Experiments

What Features Were Important?	Did This Change for Experiment #1?	Did This Change for Experiment #2?	Did This Change for Experiment #3?	Did This Change for Experiment #4?
Water				
Sunlight				
Soil				
Food/Nutrients				

Name:______________________________ Date:______________

Handout 10C

Model for a Data Table

	Height of Plant	Number of Leaves	Color	Straight Trunk	Plant Health
Observation #1 Date __________					
Observation #2 Date __________					
Observation #3 Date __________					
Observation #4 Date __________					
Observation #5 Date __________					
Observation #6 Date __________					

Lesson 11:
Follow-Up to Plant Experiments

Planning the Lesson

Instructional Purpose

- To share results of plant experiments.

Instructional Time

- 45 minutes (2 weeks after Lesson 10)

Systems Concept Generalizations

- Systems have parts (elements).
- Systems have boundaries.
- Systems have inputs and outputs.
- A system's elements interact with each other and a system's inputs.

Key Science Concepts

- Plants have basic needs, including air, water, nutrients, and light.
- Plants are dependent on other living things and their surroundings for survival.
- Plants have different parts that serve different functions in growth, survival, and reproduction.
- Plants undergo many changes during their life cycles.

Scientific Investigation Skills and Processes

- Create meaning.
- Tell others what was found.

Assessment "Look Fors"

- Students should be able to articulate findings.
- Students should be able to show understanding of science investigation skills and processes.
- Students should be able to discuss plants as systems.

Implementing the Lesson

1. Students share findings from each of the experiments on plant needs. Each group reports on one experiment, using the report form as the basis for the commentary.
2. Ask each group the following questions:
    - What important learning did you take away from this experiment?
    - What was the most enjoyable part of the experiment? The hardest part?
    - What new experiment might you plan to do as a group?
    - What did you learn about plants as systems?

3. Then ask the class the following questions:
    - Why are experiments difficult to do?
    - Can variables always be determined ahead of time? What else can intervene to affect results?

Lesson 12: Independent and Small-Group Investigation

Planning the Lesson

Instructional Purpose

- To share student projects on seeds.
- To share resolutions to Professor Blackwell's work on using plants for fuel.

Instructional Time

- 45 minutes

Systems Concept Generalizations

- Systems have parts (elements).
- Systems have boundaries.
- Systems have inputs and outputs.
- A system's elements interact with each other and a system's inputs.

Key Science Concepts

- Plants have different parts that serve different functions in growth, survival, and reproduction.
- Plants undergo many changes during their life cycles.

Scientific Investigation Skills and Processes

- Make observations.
- Ask questions.
- Learn more.
- Design and conduct experiments.
- Create meaning.
- Tell others what was found.

Assessment "Look Fors"

- Students should be able to share knowledge and understandings about their seed collection.
- Students should be able to make accurate inferences about whether plants can be used to fuel cars.

Materials/Resources/Equipment

- Slide of Handout 12A (Concept Map of a Seed)
- Chart or slide of Handout 6C (Blank Need to Know Board)
- Resources gathered to answer the question: "Can plants help fuel cars?"

Implementing the Lesson

Part I

1. Set up student seed collection displays around the room (from Lesson 9). Ask three students to describe their displays, using the Experimental Report Form (Handout 9B) as an outline for their presentation.
2. Ask the entire class the following questions:
   - What other types of seeds from what we have just heard about did you collect?
   - What different findings did you have from your observations?
   - Was your hypothesis about seeds accurate? Why or why not?
   - How can you describe a "seed" as a system?
   - What did you learn from doing the seed collection project?

Part II

3. Have students draw a concept map of a seed. Discuss the drawings as a class. Students should match their drawing to the concept map in Handout 12A. How are they similar and different?
4. Now ask students to work with you on a new blank Need to Know Board (Handout 6C) based on their understanding of Professor Blackwell's problem. Fill in the question for discussion: "Can plants help fuel cars?" Ask students to brainstorm what they currently know about the question and what they need to know. Students should write new questions about what they need to know.
5. Provide resource information gathered by the librarian for students to discuss in small groups in order to answer any questions they still have about plants and how they can provide fuel. Divide questions by groups.
6. Have groups report their answers and add to the board for in-class resolution.

Concluding and Extending the Lesson

Log Prompt

- If you were Professor Blackwell, what would you have done differently in respect to your research on plants?

What to Do at Home

- Students should develop a set of new questions they now have about plants, designing an experiment, and understanding systems. They should bring their questions to class for the unit wrap-up.

Name:______________________________ Date:______________

Handout 12A

Concept Map of a Seed

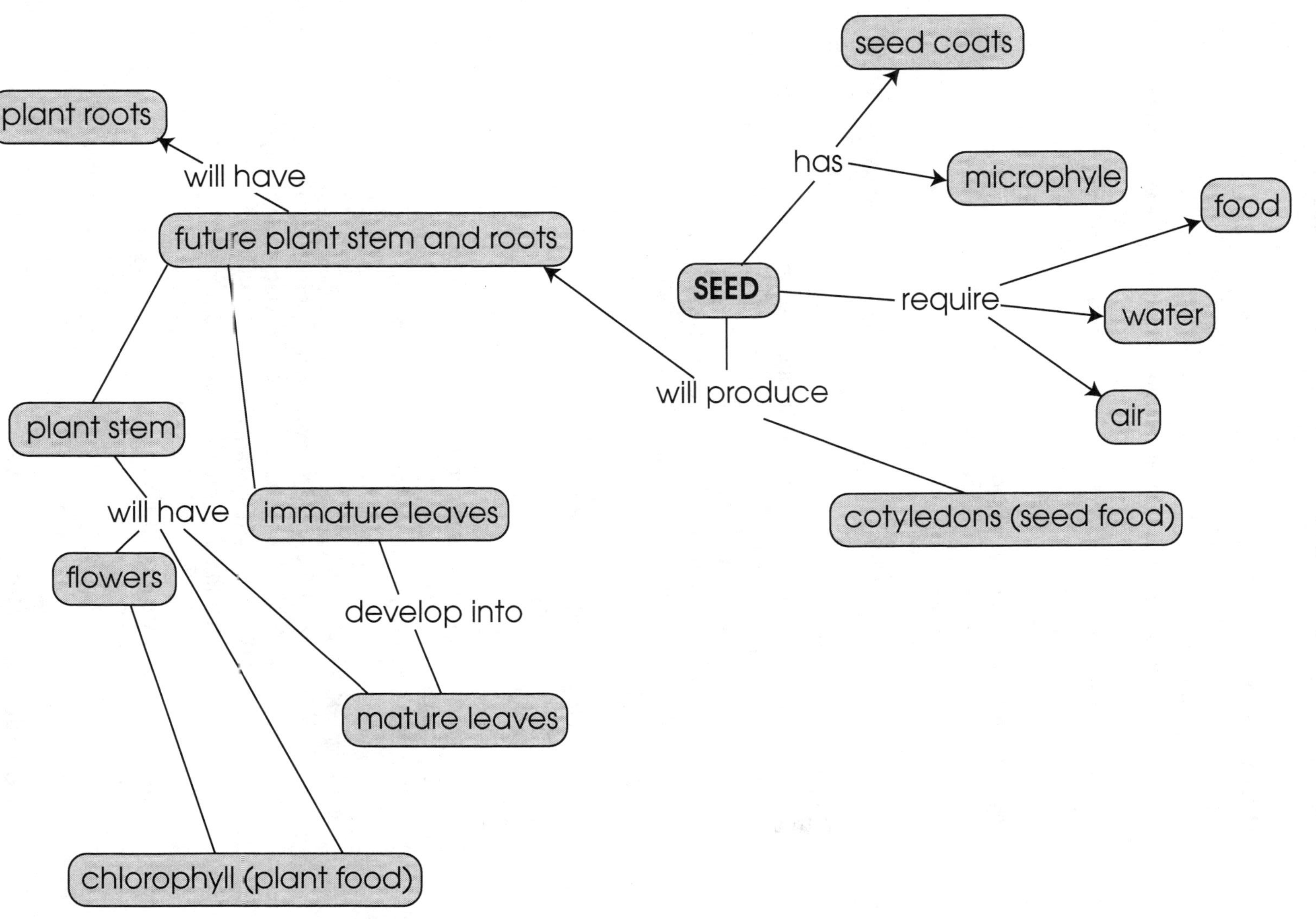

© Prufrock Press Inc. • *Budding Botanists*
This page may be photocopied or reproduced with permission for classroom use only.

Lesson 13: Wrap It Up!

Planning the Lesson

Instructional Purpose

- To summarize content, scientific process, and conceptual understanding.

Instructional Time

- 45 minutes

Systems Concept Generalizations

- Systems have parts (elements).
- Systems have boundaries.
- Systems have inputs and outputs.
- A system's elements interact with each other and a system's inputs.

Key Science Concepts

- Plants have basic needs, including air, water, nutrients, and light.
- Plants have different parts that serve different functions in growth, survival, and reproduction.
- Plants undergo many changes during their life cycles.
- Different plants have different characteristics.
- Plants cause changes in the environment where they live.

Scientific Investigation Skills and Processes

- Make observations.
- Ask questions.
- Learn more.
- Design and conduct experiments.
- Create meaning.
- Tell others what was found.

Assessment "Look Fors"

- Students should be able to draw a concept map for a term used in the unit.
- Students should be able to describe the scientific investigative process and explain its application to plants.
- Students should be able to describe a plant system.

Materials/Resources/Equipment

- Student log books
- Computer (optional)

Implementing the Lesson

1. Review questions that students bring in from yesterday's homework assignment.
2. Wrap up the student log books:

- Review the log books with the students. Show them a segment from Darwin's log or Salk's log to give them the idea that all scientists use logs in their work. Discuss any questions about log entries that they have.

3. Wrap up the problem:
   - Revisit the original problem scenario and yesterday's activity: How have we done with it as a scientific team?
   - Review the log entries.
   - Make sure students understand that finding a solution often takes scientists many years. Explain that Professor Blackwell's work could be the foundation for other scientists to explore.
   - Discuss the process that is used to research a solution, test a solution, and get it to market. Explain that the time that lapses between discovery and end product is very long.

4. Wrap up the investigation process, using the following:
   - Review the Experimental Report Form (Handout 9B) steps. Do a demonstration, using a paper cup to cover a plant. How long would it take the plant to die? What would they predict? Work through the steps and discuss.
   - What questions have we asked?
   - What data sources have we used in the unit?
   - What types of hypotheses have we made?
   - What were some of our findings?
   - What did we learn from the investigations?

5. Wrap up the systems concept:
   - Have students describe a plant system in their own words and draw one, then share their description with a partner and discuss. Ask three pairs to share in the room.
   - Ask the students: How are the descriptions and drawings similar and different? Can we add components to the plant system that we have studied?
   - Create a class plant system to hang in the room.

Concluding and Extending the Lesson

Concluding Questions

- In what ways has your thinking about plants and systems changed based on our investigations?

What to Do at Home

- Have students take their log books, seedlings, and other unit materials home. Tell them to share what they have learned with their parents.

Postassessment

Instructional Purpose

- To assess student knowledge of the concept of systems, student skills in the scientific process, and student understanding of unit content about plants.

Instructional Time

- Concept assessment: 30 minutes
- Scientific process assessment: 20 minutes
- Content assessment: 20 minutes

Materials/Resources/Equipment

- Copies of postassessments (Postassessment for Systems Concept, Postassessment for Science Content, Postassessment for Scientific Process)
- Rubrics 1–3 (see Preassessment section) and Exemplar Answers for Systems Concept, Exemplar Concept Maps of Plants, and Exemplar Answers for Scientific Process for scoring
- Pencils
- Large chart paper
- Drawing paper for each student

Implementing the Lesson

1. Give each student a copy of the postassessments to complete in the order noted above. The assessments should take no more than 70 minutes total. However, it is recommended that teachers administer only *one* postassessment per day. Explain that the assessment will be used to see how much students have learned during the unit.
2. Use the rubrics contained in the preassessment sections for concept, scientific process, and content to score the assessments. Exemplar answers for the postassessment for systems concept have been provided on p. 110, for the science content postassessment on p. 113, and for the scientific process postassessment on p. 116.

Name:______________________________ Date:____________

Postassessment for the Systems Concept

1. Give *five* examples of things that are "systems."

____

____

____

____

____

2. Draw *one* example of a system that you know.

3. Label at least *five* features of your system.

4. What are *three* things you can say about *all* systems?

All systems ______________________________.

All systems ______________________________.

All systems ______________________________.

Exemplar Answers for Systems Concept

Note: Student answers may vary; these are simply to provide samples of quality postassessment answers to aid in scoring.

High Score

1. Give five examples of things that are "systems."
   Plane, car, computer, tree, body

2. Draw one example of a system that you know.
   A tree

3. Label at least five features of your system.
   Branch, Leaves, Trunk, Root, Dirt

4. What are three things you can say about all systems?
   They have inputs and outputs. They have boundaries. They have interaction.

Medium Score

1. Give five examples of things that are "systems."
   Toy car, people, shoes, paper, whiteboard

2. Draw one example of a system that you know.
   A toy car

3. Label at least five features of your system.
   Blank

4. What are three things you can say about all systems?
   They have wheels. They have doors. They have windows.

Low Score

1. Give five examples of things that are "systems."
   Car, story, tree, school

2. Draw one example of a system that you know.
   Blank

3. Label at least five features of your system.
   Blank

4. What are three things you can say about all systems?
   Car helps you go anywhere. School helps you learn. Story helps you buy.

Postassessment for Science Content

Directions for Use: Read the following paragraph to the students.

Today I would like you to think about all the things you know about plants. Think about the words you would use and the pictures you could draw to make a concept map. Think about the connections you can make. On your concept map paper, draw in pictures and words all that you know about plants. You will be drawing a concept map similar to those you have done before.

Name:______________________________ Date:_______________

Concept Map
Plants

Exemplar Concept Maps of Plants

High Score

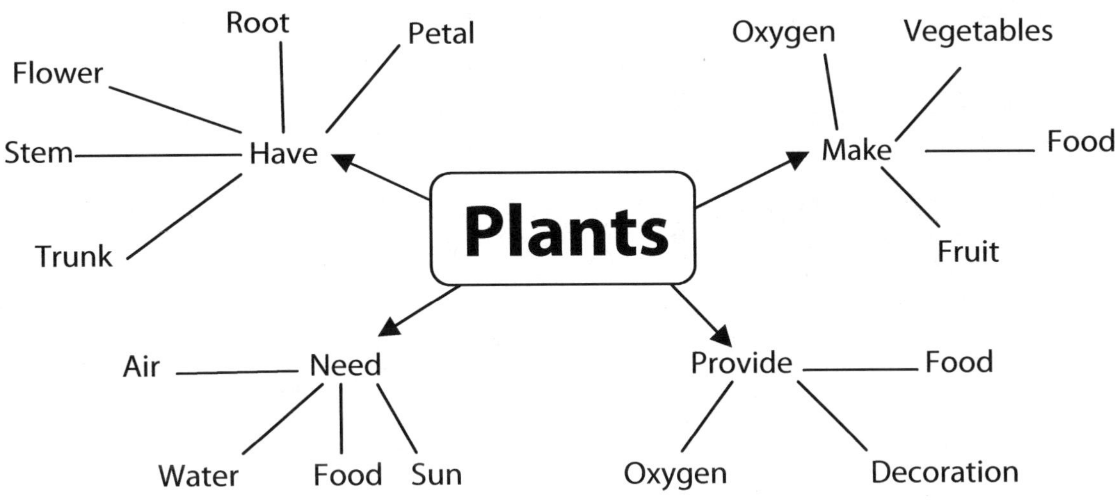

Medium Score

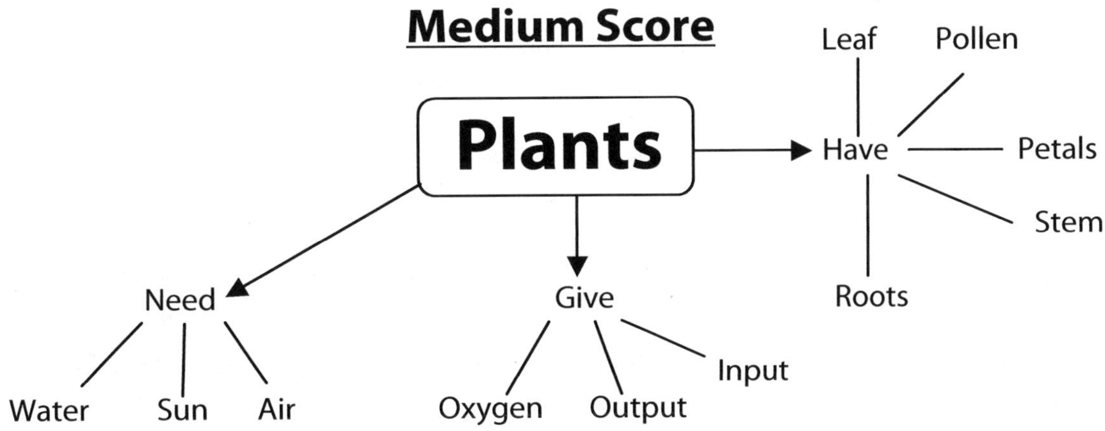

Low Score

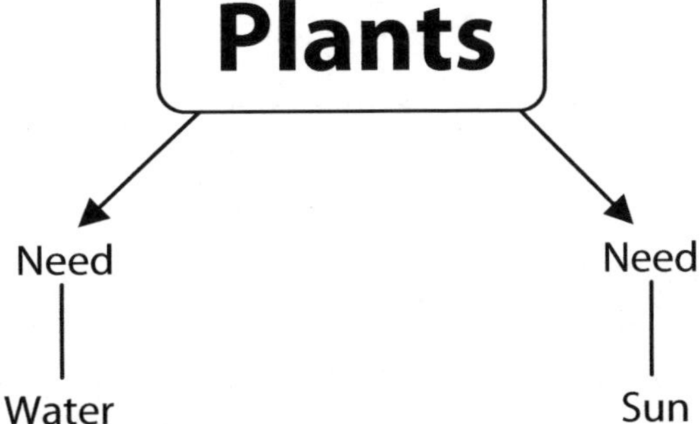

Name:______________________________ Date:__________

Postassessment for Scientific Process

Directions: How would you study the question: How much water do plants need? Describe an experiment to test this question that includes the following:

1. Prediction regarding the question (How much water do plants need?):

   I predict that____

   ____

   ____

   ____.

2. What materials will be needed to conduct the experiment?

   ________________________ ________________________

   ________________________ ________________________

   ________________________ ________________________

3. What steps must be taken to conduct the experiment and *in what order*?

   a. ____

   b. ____

   c. ____

   d. ____

   e. ____

Name:________________________________ Date:____________

4. What data do you want to collect and how should it be recorded?

What will I collect?	How will I record it?

5. How do the data help me decide if my prediction is correct? Explain.

____

____

____

____

Exemplar Answers for Scientific Process

High Score

1. What is your prediction regarding the question: "How much water do plants need?"
   They should need a lot of water.

2. What materials will be needed to conduct the experiment?
   Plant, water, somewhere outside, sunshine

3. What steps must be taken to conduct the experiment and in what order?
   a) Go outside. b) Get a plant. c) Put it in the sun. d) Get some water.

4. What data do you want to collect and how should it be recorded?
   What will I collect? I think I'm going to learn about plants. When you give a plant some water it grows bigger and stronger and it might not really die.
   How will I record it? I will write on a piece of paper what I just learned.

5. How do the data help me decide if my prediction is correct? Explain.
   I think that is correct because this is what I learned about.

Medium Score

1. What is your prediction regarding the question: "How much water do plants need?"
   ½ cup of water and with water the flowers grow.

2. What materials will be needed to conduct the experiment?
   Water, sun, cup, soil, ½ cup, seed

3. What steps must be taken to conduct the experiment and in what order?
   a) First you put the seed on the dirt. b) Plant the flower with water. c) Then it will grow.

4. What data do you want to collect and how should it be recorded?
   Blank

5. How do the data help me decide if my prediction is correct? Explain.
   Blank

Low Score

1. What is your prediction regarding the question: "How much water do plants need?"
   ½

2. What materials will be needed to conduct the experiment?
   Bucket, sun, water, dirt, oxygen, soil

3. What steps must be taken to conduct the experiment and in what order?
   a) Bucket, b) Soil, c) Oxygen, d) Sun, e) Air

4. What data do you want to collect and how should it be recorded?
   Drew a picture of a flower

5. How do the data help me decide if my prediction is correct? Explain.
   Because you need water, makes it grow, it goes through the stem

Appendix A
Concept Paper on Systems

By Beverly T. Sher, Ph.D.

This paper was adapted from: Sher, B. T. (2004). Systems. In J. VanTassel-Baska (Ed.), *Science key concepts*. Williamsburg, VA: Center for Gifted Education, The College of William and Mary.

A system is a collection of things and processes that interact with each other and together constitute a meaningful whole. Examples from the realm of science include atoms, chemical reaction systems, individual cells, organs, organ systems, organisms, ecosystems, solar systems, and galaxies; nonscience examples include sewer systems, political systems, the banking system, transportation systems, and so on. All systems share certain properties. These include:

1. Systems have identifiable elements.
2. Systems have definable boundaries.
3. Most systems receive input in the form of material or information from outside their boundaries and generate output to the world outside their boundaries.
4. The interactions of a system's elements with each other and their response to input from outside the system combine to determine the overall nature and behavior of the system.

Figure A1 provides an illustration of how systems work.

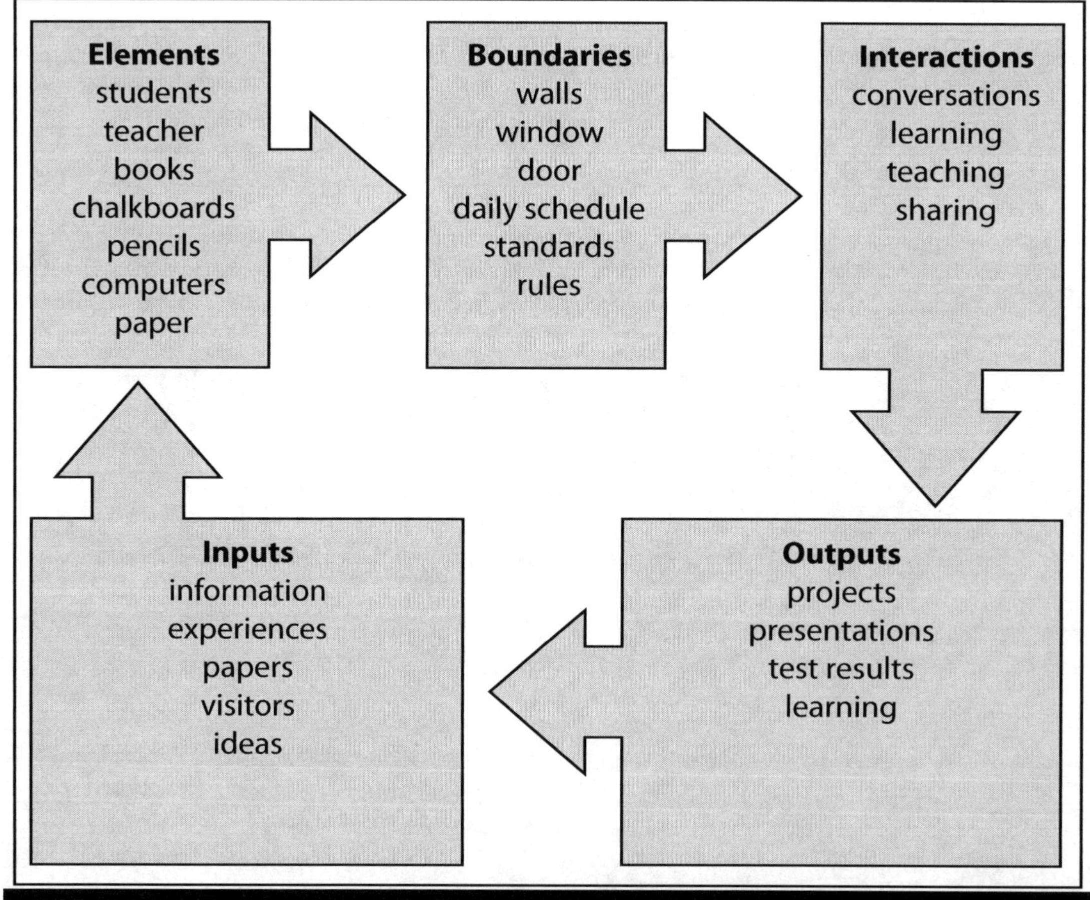

Figure A1. How systems work.

Systems are made up of identifiable elements and processes. The elements comprising an ecosystem, for example, include all of the organisms present as well as all of the physical features of the area that the ecosystem occupies. The elements of a forest ecosystem would include the different trees, bushes, and smaller plants; the insects, birds, and other animals present; the nature of the terrain; the quality of the soil; the availability of water; the weather; and so on. Defining the elements of an ecosystem thoroughly is a large task. Similarly, the elements of nonscience systems are clearly definable. A school system would include all of the physical property appertaining to the schools and their administration: schools, playgrounds, buses, administration buildings, and so on. It also includes all of the teachers, pupils, administrators, and (ideally) parents.

The boundaries of systems also must be defined. The boundaries of an ecosystem are defined physically: they are the boundaries of the territory that it occupies. Thus, the boundary of a forest ecosystem is the edge of the forest. An ecosystem's boundaries can be drawn somewhat arbitrarily; one can speak of a backyard ecosystem or of the planetary ecosystem. The first ecosystem would thus be an element of the second ecosystem. The appropriate choice of boundaries for an ecosystem depends on the phenomena that one wishes to study: To study global warming, it is necessary to include the whole planet, but a study of the effects of man on the alpine tundra could involve only a single mountaintop. Similarly, the boundaries of nonscience systems can be defined in somewhat arbitrary ways, depending on the nature of the process under study. The boundaries of a school system could be chosen to exclude neighboring systems and the federal government. Although all of these elements can affect the school system, they really are not integral to its behavior.

Drawing the boundaries of a system appropriately can reveal much about its nature and behavior. Including phenomena and elements that are irrelevant to the properties under study will make understanding the system unnecessarily difficult. For example, including detailed consideration of the daily actions of members of the Williamsburg City Council in a study of the overall behavior of the American political system adds variables that are probably insignificant for the behavior of the system as a whole and therefore makes the study of the system unnecessarily difficult. Excluding the press from the system, however, probably decreases the understanding of the system, even though the press is not a formally defined branch of government. Although the press could be considered as an external actor that produces input into the system, in practice the actions of the press are so tightly intermeshed with the actions of those that run the government that excluding the press from the government system would make understanding the system more difficult rather than less.

As discussed in *Science for All Americans* (Rutherford & Ahlgren, 1990), one of the best examples of the importance of properly defining the boundaries and elements of an experimental system is Louis Pasteur's elegant experimental solution for the problem of the spontaneous generation of living organisms. Before the 19th century, it was widely believed that living organisms arose spontaneously from nonliving matter, without benefit of the action of other living things. Rats and mice were thought to arise spontaneously from old rags, maggots from old meat. In the 1800s, Louis Pasteur approached this problem experimentally and resolved it. He showed that if flies were kept from contact with meat, no maggots subsequently arose from it; and if meat broth was boiled and then kept in sealed flasks or in flasks that allowed the entry of air but not of dust particles, then the broth did not spoil. By drawing the boundaries of his experimental system to exclude certain elements (namely flies and bacteria), Pasteur proved that meat alone was insufficient to generate maggots and meat broth alone did not spoil. Thus, the doctrine of spontaneous generation was laid to rest.

Another example of the importance of correctly understanding the boundaries and elements integral to a system comes from the controversy over the origin of life on Earth. The science of thermodynamics has been used (inappropriately) to argue that life could not have evolved from nonliving chemicals through simple life forms and up to the many complex forms that we see today; this argument is based on a misunderstanding of the boundaries of the system in which life evolved and an incomplete understanding of thermodynamics. Thermodynamics is the science that sets the limits on energy efficiency and possible outcome of physical and chemical processes. The three laws of thermodynamics can be summarized as follows:

1. Energy can neither be created nor destroyed, only transferred or changed from one form to another.
2. In an irreversible process, the entropy (degree of disorder) of the universe increases; only in a reversible process will it stay constant. The entropy of the universe cannot decrease.
3. At the temperature absolute zero, the entropy of perfect crystals and compounds is zero.

The second law of thermodynamics has been misused to argue that life could not possibly have evolved, because over time the complexity of living things has increased, and hence the system of life on Earth has become more ordered, not more disordered. The basic flaw in this argument is that its proponents have neglected to include the sun in their calculations. Solar energy is the source of most of the energy used by organisms; thus the thermodynamic properties of the sun must be included in the system. The net entropy of the sun has increased by a degree that is orders of magnitude greater than the degree of entropy decrease caused by the origin and actions of all life on Earth; thus the entropy of the universe has increased, as it theoretically should.

A third fundamental property of systems is that they can receive input from and act on the world outside their boundaries. Input into a school system, for example, includes federal financial and material assistance. Output from a school system includes educated students. Input into an ecosystem includes things such as solar energy; output from an ecosystem includes things such as carbon dioxide released into the atmosphere as a result of animal respiration and oxygen released by plants.

The final fundamental property of a system is that its overall behavior depends on the properties and interactions of its parts. For example, understanding the behavior of an ecosystem (e.g., whether it is stable or likely to change, whether it is delicate and sensitive to the incursions of man, or whether it can survive human influence with few changes) depends upon understanding the roles of the different elements in the ecosystem and their interactions. Thus prediction of the number of deer that can be safely hunted in a given area depends upon knowing how fast they reproduce, which wild predators are present and what percentage of the deer population they kill, whether disease is present in the deer population and likely to reduce numbers substantially, which plants the deer use for food and how many deer the plant population can support without being reduced too far to replace itself, and so on.

This dependence of the behavior of the whole system on the properties and interactions of its parts also is seen in nonscience systems. The behavior of the federal government depends on the actions and motivations of its members, their interactions with each other, and their reactions to input from their constituents and from the outside world. The behavior of the local sewer system depends on the amount of material it receives, the age of the pipes, the capacity of the treatment plant, and so on. Attempting to understand the behavior of the whole system based on the nature of its parts is the essence of the philosophy of reductionism, which has been a highly successful approach to the study of systems in general.

Rationale for Teaching the Concept

The understanding of the behavior of one system will help understanding of other systems. Defining the elements, boundaries, inputs, and outputs of a system helps to understand its behavior as a whole. Once a child has learned to do this for a simple system, he or she will be able to apply the process to other, more complex systems. This will help the child understand the scientific process, as setting up successful experiments involves determining which elements should be included and paying close attention to the inputs and outputs of the system; varying the elements present in the experimental system may well change the experimental outcome in ways that illuminate the functioning of the system. More generally, the study of certain scientific systems will deepen a child's understanding of the world around him or her. Every child should have some understanding of the ecosystem of which he or she is an element and the solar system in which he or she resides.

Suggested Applications

There are two different ways to approach the concept of systems with children. The first involves weaving it into the experimental work that they do in the course of their science studies. Defining the experimental system thoroughly and paying attention to the essential variables in the system and excluding the others from consideration are activities critical to any lab science course. The second approach to the concept involves teaching them about some basic scientific systems. Many scientific systems are accessible to children, at least at a simple level. These include systems from many disciplines, including chemistry, geology, biology, and astronomy, as listed (albeit in incomplete fashion) below:

Biology

- ecosystems
- organ systems
- organisms: physiology, behavior

Chemistry

- chemical reaction systems

Geology

- the planet Earth as a geological system: plate tectonics and its manifestations
- geologic change in mountain ranges, river systems, and the like

Meteorology

- weather systems

Astronomy

- solar systems
- galaxies
- Earth-moon system

Problem-Based Learning

The following is an example of a problem-based learning situation that could be used to illustrate the system concept.

The Problem: You own a gardening store. Several townspeople have signed a petition asking you to stop selling some of your products. What should you do?

Areas for students to explore:

1. The garden as a system: look at the interactions of the plants and animals present and seek to minimize animal and disease destruction of the plants.
2. Organic farming techniques
3. Resistant plant varieties
4. Plant varieties that are suitable for the local area's soil conditions, sun-shade conditions, and weather patterns.

Activities for Students: Plant and tend two gardens: an organic garden and a garden in which chemical fertilizers, insecticides, and herbicides are used. Record the amount and kinds of work needed to maintain each; the amounts of chemicals used in the chemical garden; and the yields of the different fruits, vegetables, and flowers planted in each. Report results.

Appendix B
Teaching Models

Introduction to the Teaching Models

Several teaching models are incorporated into the Project Clarion units. These models ensure emphasis on unit outcomes and support student understanding of the concepts and processes that are the focus of each unit. Teachers should become familiar with these models and how to use them before teaching the unit. The models are listed below and outlined in the pages that follow.

1. Frayer Model of Vocabulary Development
2. Taba Model of Concept Development
3. Concept Mapping
4. Wheel of Scientific Investigation and Reasoning

Frayer Model of Vocabulary Development

The Frayer Model (Frayer, Frederick, & Klausmeier, 1969) provides students with a graphic organizer that asks them to think about and describe the meaning of a word or concept. This process enables them to strengthen their understanding of vocabulary words. Through the model, students are required to consider the important characteristics of the word and to provide examples and nonexamples of the concept. This model has similarities to the Taba Model of Concept Development (1962).

In introducing the Frayer Model to your students, demonstrate its use on large chart paper. Begin with a word all students know, such as rock, umbrella, or shoe, placing it on the graphic model. First, ask the students to define the word in their own words. Record a definition that represents their common knowledge. Next, ask students to give specific characteristics of the word/concept or facts they know about it. Record these ideas. Then ask students to offer examples of the idea and then nonexamples to finish the graphic (see Figure B1).

Another way to use the Frayer Model is to provide students with examples and nonexamples and ask them to consider what word or concept is being analyzed. You can provide similar exercises by filling in some portions of the graphic and asking students to complete the remaining sections.

As students share ideas, note the level of understanding of the group and of individual students. As the unit is taught, certain vocabulary words may need this type of expanded thinking to support student readiness for using the vocabulary in the science activities. You may want students to maintain individual notebooks of words so that they can refer back to them in their work.

Taba Model of Concept Development

Each Project Clarion unit supports the development of a specific macroconcept (change or systems). The concept development model, based upon the work of Hilda Taba (1962), supports student learning of the macroconcept. The model involves both inductive and deductive reasoning processes. Used as an early lesson in the unit, the model focuses on the creation of generalizations about the macroconcept from a student-derived list of created concept examples. The model includes a series

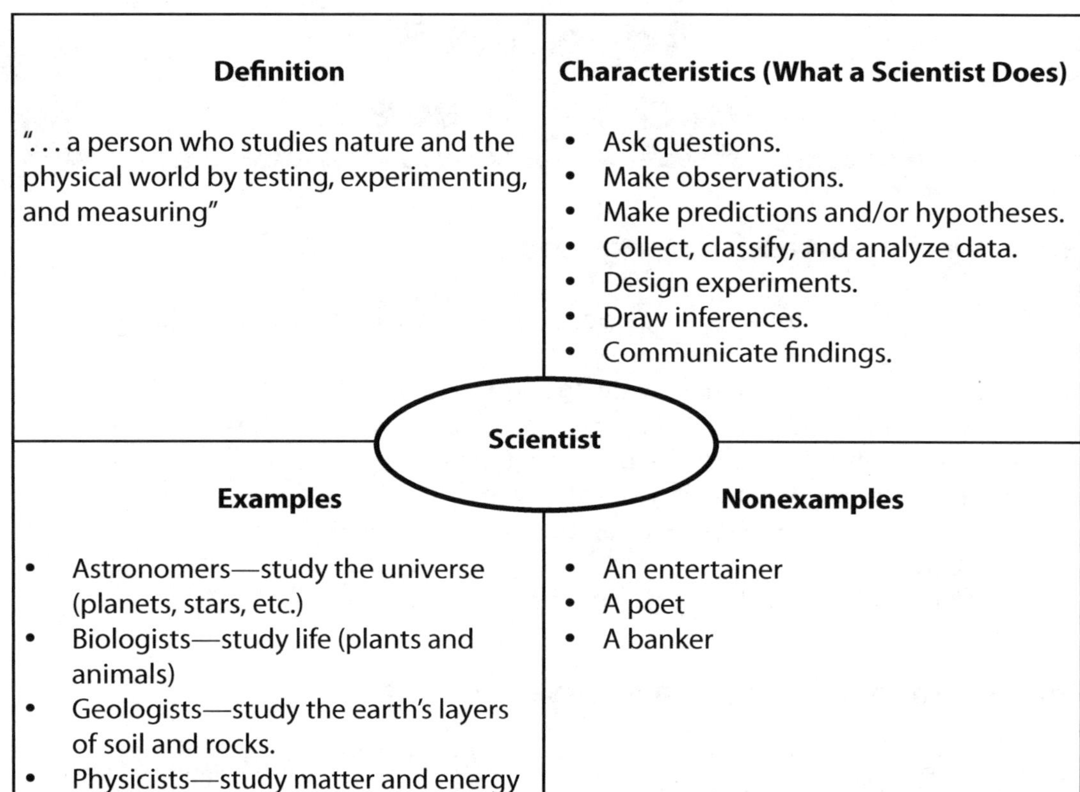

Figure B1. Completed graphic organizer for Frayer Model.

of steps, in which each step involves student participation. Students begin with a broad concept, determine specific examples of the broad concept, create appropriate categorization systems, cite nonexamples of the concept, establish generalizations based on their understanding, and then apply the generalizations to their readings and other situations.

The model generally is most effective when small groups of students work through each step, with whole-class debriefing following each stage of the process. However, with primary-age students, additional teacher guidance may be necessary, especially for the later stages of the model. The steps of the model are outlined below, using the unit concept of change.

1. Students generate examples of the concept of change, derived from their own understanding and experiences with change in the world. Teachers should encourage students to provide at least 15–20 examples; a class list may be created out of the small-group lists to lengthen the set of changes students have to work with.
2. Students then group their changes into categories. This process allows students to search for interrelatedness and to organize their thinking. It often is helpful to have individual examples written on cards so that the categorization may occur physically as well as mentally or in writing. Students should then explain their reasoning for their categorization system and seek clarification from each other as a whole group. Teachers should ensure that all examples have been accounted for in the categorization system established.
3. Students then generate a list of nonexamples of the concept of change. Teachers may begin this step with the direction, "Now list examples of things that *do not change*." Encourage students to think carefully about their

nonexamples and discuss ideas within their groups. Each group should list five to six nonexamples.

4. The students next determine generalizations about the concept of change, using their lists of examples, categories, and nonexamples. Teachers should then share the unit generalizations and relate valid student generalizations to the unit list. Both lists should be posted in the room throughout the course of the unit.
5. During the unit, students are asked to identify specific examples of the generalizations from their own readings, or to describe how the concept applies to a given situation about which they have read. Students also are asked to apply the generalizations to their own writings and their own lives. Several lessons employ a chart that lists several of the generalizations and asks students to supply examples specifically related to the reading or activity of that lesson.

Concept Mapping

A concept map is a graphic representation of one's knowledge on a particular topic. Concept maps support learning, teaching, and evaluation (Novak & Gowin, 1984). Students clarify and extend their own thinking about a topic. Teachers find concept mapping useful for envisioning the scope of a lesson or unit. They also use student-developed concept maps as a way of measuring their progress. Meaningful concept maps often begin with a particular question (focus question) about a topic, event, or object.

Concept maps were developed in 1972 by Dr. Joseph Novak at Cornell University as part of his research about young children's understanding of science concepts. Students were interviewed by researchers who recorded their responses. The researchers sought an effective way to identify changes in students' understanding over time. Novak and his research colleagues began to represent the students' conceptual understanding in concept maps because learning takes place through the assimilation of new concepts and propositions into existing conceptual and propositional frameworks.

Concept maps show concepts and relationships between them. (See the sample concept map in Figure B2.) The concepts are contained within boxes or oval shapes and the connections between concepts are represented by lines with linking words.

Concepts are the students' perceived ideas generalized from particular experiences. Sometimes the concepts placed on the map may contain more than one word. Words placed on the line link words or phrases. The propositions contain two or more concepts connected by linking words or phrases to form a meaningful statement.

The youngest students may view and develop concept maps making basic connections. They may begin with two concepts joined by a linking word. These "sentences" (propositions) become the building blocks for concept maps. Older students may begin to make multiple connections immediately as they develop their maps.

As students map their knowledge base, they begin to represent their conceptual understanding in a hierarchical manner. The broadest, most inclusive concepts often are found at the top of a concept map. More specific concepts and examples then follow.

Each Project Clarion unit contains an overview concept map, showing the essential knowledge included in the lessons and the connections students should be able to make as a result of their experiences within the unit. This overview may be useful as a classroom poster that the teacher and students may refer to throughout the unit.

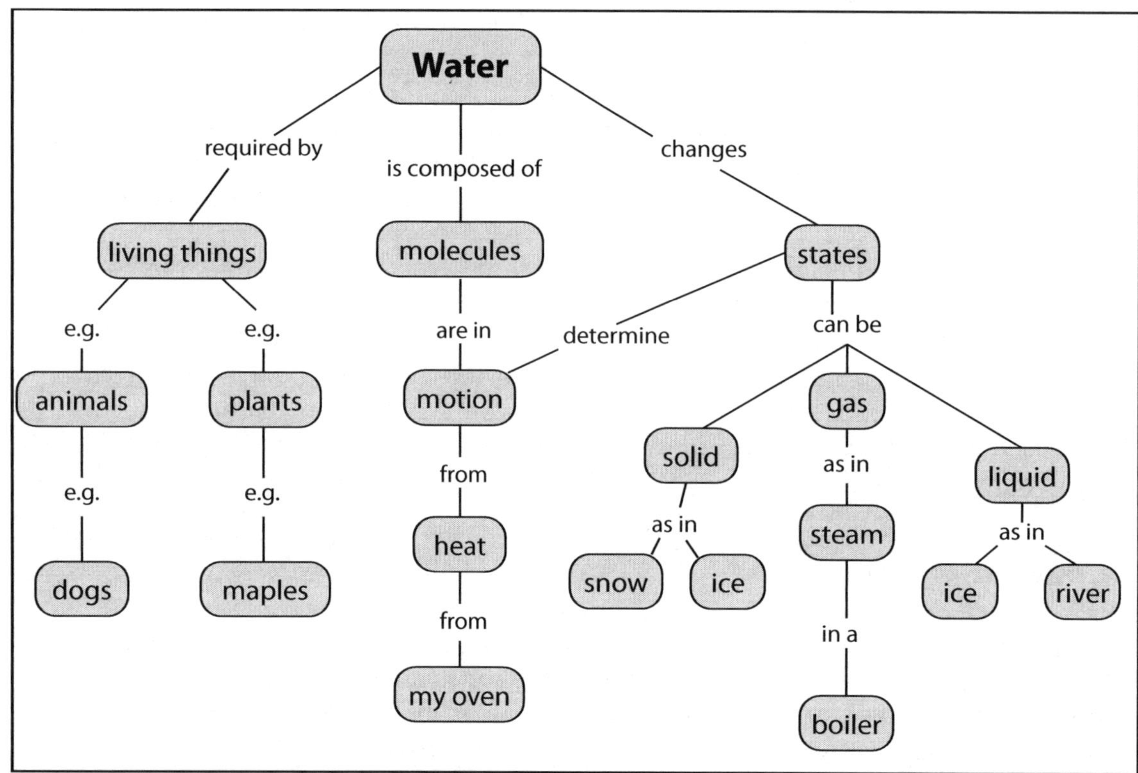

Figure B2. A concept map showing a student's understanding of water.

Note. Adapted from Novak and Gowin (1984).

Strategies to Prepare Students for Concept Mapping

The following strategies can be incorporated to help prepare your students for concept mapping activities (Novak & Gowin, 1984).

What Do Words Mean?

1. Ask students to picture in their minds some common words (e.g., water, tree, door, box, pencil, dog). Start with "object" words, saying them one at a time, allowing time for students to picture each of them.
2. Create a class list of object words, asking students to name other objects they can picture in their minds to add to the list.
3. Next create a list of event words (e.g., jumping, running, eating). Ask students to envision each of these in their minds and encourage them to contribute to the class list of event words.
4. Give students a few words that are likely to be unfamiliar to most of them, asking if they can see a picture in their mind. These words should be short (e.g., data, cell, prey, inertia). You might include a few simple words in another language. Ask students if they have any mind pictures.
5. Discuss the fact that words are useful to us because they convey meaning. This only happens when people can form a picture in their mind that represents the meaning they connect with the word.

What Is a Concept?

1. Introduce the word *concept* and explain that concept is the word we use to mean some kind of object or event we can picture in our mind. Refer back to the word lists previously developed as you discuss the word and ask if these are concepts. Can students see a picture in their mind for each of them? Let students know that when they come upon a word they do not know well enough to form a picture, they will just need to learn the concept associated with that new word.
2. Provide each table with picture cards and ask students to take turns at their table naming some of the concepts included in the card.

What Are Linking Words?

1. Prepare a list of words such as *the, is, are, when, that, then*. Ask students if they can see a picture in their mind for each of these words. Explain that these are not concept words. These are linking words we use when we speak or write to link concept words together into sentences that have special meaning. Ask students if they have any words to add to the list. Label the list "Linking Words."
2. Hold up two picture cards (sky and blue) and give students a sample sentence ("The sky is blue.") Ask students to tell you the concept words and the linking words in your sentence. Give another example.
3. Give each pair of students a few picture cards. Ask the students to work with partners to pick up two cards and then develop a sentence that links the two cards. They should take turns, with one partner making the sentence and the other identifying the concepts and the linking words. Ask them to repeat this a few times and then have several partners share their sentences.
4. Explain to students that it is easy to make up sentences and to read sentences where the printed labels (words) are familiar to them. Explain that reading and writing sentences is like making a link between two things (concepts) they already know. Practice this idea during reading time, asking students to find a sentence and analyze it for concepts and linking words.

Wheel of Scientific Investigation and Reasoning

All scientists work to improve our knowledge and understanding of the world. In the process of scientific inquiry, scientists connect evidence with logical reasoning. Scientists also apply their imaginations as they devise hypotheses and explanations that make sense of the evidence. Students can strengthen their understanding of particular science topics through investigations that cause them to employ evidence gathering, logical reasoning, and creativity. The Wheel of Scientific Investigation and Reasoning contains the specific processes involved in scientific inquiry to guide students' thinking and actions.

Make Observations

Scientists make careful observations and try things out. They must describe things as accurately as possible so that they can compare their observations from one time to another and so that they can compare their observations with those of other scientists. Scientists use their observations to form questions for investigation.

Ask Questions

Scientific investigations usually are initiated through a problem to be solved or a question asked. Selecting just the right question or clearly defining the problem to be addressed is critical to the investigation process.

Learn More

To clarify their questions, scientists learn more by reviewing bodies of scientific knowledge documented in text and previously conducted investigations. Also, when scientists get conflicting information they make fresh observations and insights that may result in revision of the previously formed question. By learning more, scientists can design and conduct more effective experiments or build upon previously conducted experiments.

Design and Conduct an Experiment

Scientists use their collection of relevant evidence, their reasoning, and their imagination to develop a hypothesis. Sometimes scientists have more than one possible explanation for the same set of observations and evidence. Often when additional observations and testing are completed, scientists modify current scientific knowledge.

To test out hypotheses, scientists design experiments that will enable them to control conditions so that their results will be reliable. Scientists repeat their experiments, doing it the same way it was done before and expecting to get very similar, although not exact, results. It is important to control conditions in order to make comparisons. Scientists sometimes are not sure what will happen because they don't know everything that might be having an effect on the experiment's outcome.

Create Meaning From the Experiment

Scientists analyze the data that are collected from the experiment to add to the existing body of scientific knowledge. They organize their data using data tables and graphs and then make inferences from the data to draw conclusions about whether their question was answered and the effectiveness of their experiments. Scientists also create meaning by comparing what they found to existing knowledge. The analysis of data often leads to identification of related questions and future experiments.

Tell Others What Was Found

In the investigation process, scientists often work as a team, sharing findings with each other so that they may benefit from the results. Initially, individual team members complete their own work and draw their own conclusions.

One way to introduce the wheel to students is to provide them with the graphic model (see Figure B3) and ask them to tell one reason why each section of the wheel is important to scientific investigation.

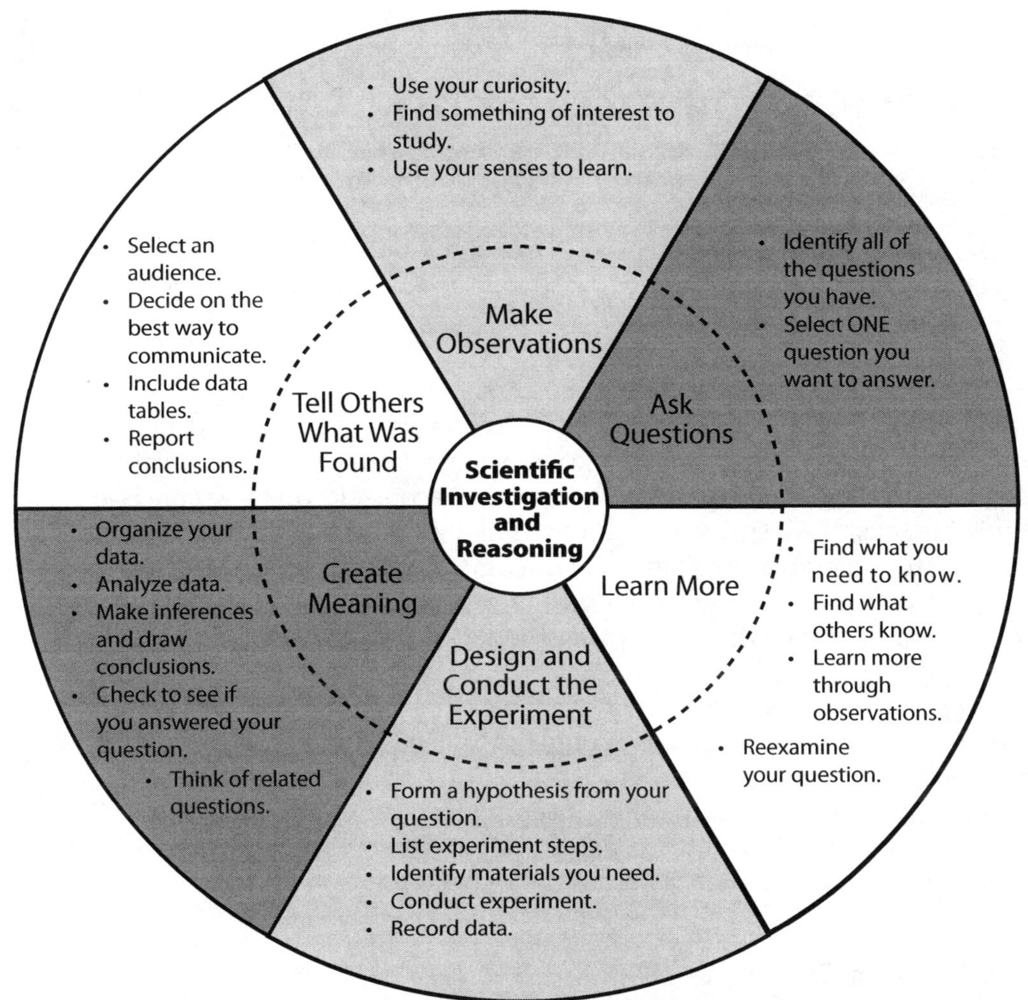

Figure B3. Wheel of Scientific Investigation and Reasoning model.

Note. Adapted from Kramer (1987).

Appendix C
Basic Concepts in Early Childhood

By Bruce A. Bracken, Ph.D., and Elizabeth Crawford

This paper was adapted from: Bracken, B. A., & Crawford, E. (2009). *Basic concepts in early childhood educational standards: A 50 state review*. Manuscript submitted for publication.

This paper presents the authors' conceptualization of basic concepts as the foundation of early childhood knowledge (e.g., Bracken, 1998a). This paper's focus on basic language concepts asserts the importance of empirically supported educational interventions to reinforce systematic acquisition of basic concepts that all children must possess. These basic concepts are the language arts knowledge necessary to explore, comprehend, and discuss topical concepts in all content areas if they are to succeed in early childhood education and beyond. This fact is especially true for children from diverse cultural and linguistic backgrounds, and those with exceptionalities.

The paper provides a comprehensive table of concept knowledge (Table C1) that promotes systematic concept instruction. The table identifies foundational content and conceptual categories, subdomains of knowledge comprised within these categories, and examples of specific concepts, referred to throughout this article as "Bracken concepts" to illustrate the depth and breadth of readiness content revealed in the universe of more than 300 essential basic concepts.

The Bracken Concepts

When the Bracken Basic Concept Scale (BBCS; Bracken, 1984, 1998b, 2006a, 2006b) was conceived, it was the author's belief that there were some largely unspoken, yet agreed upon, concept-based standards in early childhood education. As this line of work progressed it became clear that there was a previously untapped universal list of essential readiness concepts and concept categories. These school readiness concepts have been shown to be valid predictors of early childhood academic success (Panter, 2000; Panter & Bracken, 2000, in press; Stebbins & McIntosh, 1996; Sterner & McCallum, 1988), cognitive development (Breen, 1985; Howell & Bracken, 1992; McIntosh, Brown, & Ross, 1995; McIntosh, Wayland, Gridley, & Barnes, 1995), language development (Bracken & Cato, 1986; Rhyner & Bracken, 1988); and, they also are ubiquitous within early childhood test directions for early childhood academic and intelligence tests (Bracken, 1986; Bracken & Brown, 2008; Cummings & Nelson, 1980; Flanagan, Alfonso, Kaminer, & Rader, 1995; Kaufman, 1978). Importantly, these concepts can be taught easily, resulting in large educational gains (Wilson, 2004) and their development proceeds along a clear developmental sequence (Bracken, 1988) across both English and Spanish languages (Bracken, et al., 1990; Bracken & Fouad, 1987).

The intent of the Bracken concept list was to identify the universe of basic concepts for parents and teachers so they might more systematically, comprehensively, and effectively teach young children. As such, the Bracken concepts represent one of the first efforts to informally establish early childhood instructional standards. The *Bracken Concept Development Program* (BBCD; Bracken, 1987) was published to provide a direct curricular link between the assessment of children's basic

Table C1
Early Childhood Conceptual Categories

Concept Category	Subdomain	Concept Examples
Colors	• Primary Colors • Secondary Colors • Tertiary Colors • Absolutes	• Red, Yellow, Blue • Orange, Green, Purple • Violet, Heather • White, Black
Letters	• Recognition - Uppercase - Lowercase • Naming - Uppercase - Lowercase • Letter Sounds • Letter Blend Sounds • Letter Production	 • Point to M, B, S, D • Point to u, v, c, b • Name this letter, W, P, R, E • Name this letter, a, e, g, k • What sound does b make? • What sound does ch make? • Print the letter X, J, Z
Numbers/ Counting	• Rote Counting • Place Counting • Number Identification - 0–9 - Double Digits - Triple Digits • Number Naming - 0–9 - Double Digits - Triple Digits • Number Production • Counting by Sets	• Counting without place value • Counting with one-to-one correspondence • Point to the 1, 5, 8, 0 • Point to the 22, 58, 95 • Point to 138, 395, 783 • What is this number? 2, 6, 9 • What is this number? 44, 78 • What is this number? 234, 783 • Print the number 6, 33, 245 • Count to 100 by 2s, 5s, 10s
Size/Comparisons	• Three-Dimensional Size • Two-Dimensional Size - Vertical - Horizontal • Comparative Sizes	• Big, Large, Small, Little • Tall, Short • Long, Short • Similar, Same, Different
Shapes	• Linear (vertical/horizontal) - Curvilinear Line - Diagonal Line - Angular Line • Two-Dimensional Shapes • Three-Dimensional Shapes	• Line, Straight • Curve • Diagonal • Angle • Circle, Square, Triangle • Sphere, Cube, Pyramid
Direction/Position	• Three-Dimensional Direction • Internal/External • Relative Proximity • Self/Other Perspective • Front/Rear • Specific Locations • Cardinal Directions	• Under, Over, Right, Left • Inside, Outside, Around • Near, Far, Beside • My Right, Your Right, My Left, Your Left • In Front of, Behind, Forward, Backward • Edge, Corner • North, South, East, West

Concept Category	Subdomain	Concept Examples
Self-/Social Awareness	• Affective Feeling • Health/Physical • Gender • Familial Relationships • Age • Mores	• Happy, Sad, Excited • Healthy, Sick, Tired • Boy, Girl, Woman, Man, Male, Female • Mother, Father, Brother • Old, Young • Right, Wrong, Correct
Texture/Material	• States of Matter • Textures • Materials • Material Characteristics • Temperatures	• Solid, Liquid, Gas • Rough, Smooth, Sharp • Cloth, Wood, Metal • Wet, Dry, Shiny, Dull • Hot, Cold
Quantity	• Part/Whole • Relative Quantity • Volume • Multiples • Comparatives/Superlatives • Fractions • Math Signs/Symbols	• Whole, Part, Piece • Lots, Few, Some, None • Full, Empty • Pair, Double, Triple, Dozen • More, Less, Most, Least • Half, One-Third • +, -, x
Time/Sequence	• Mathematical Seriation • Frequency • Natural Occurring Events • Temporal Order of Events • Temporal Absolutes • Scheduling • Speed • Relative Age • Temporal Nuances • Larger Temporal Periods	• First, Second, Third • Once, Twice • Morning, Daytime, Evening • Before, After, Finished • Never, Always • Early, Late, Next, Arriving • Fast, Slow • New, Old, Young, Old • Nearly, Just, Waiting • Days, Weeks, Months, Seasons, Years

Note. Adapted from Kramer (1987).

concept knowledge and conceptual instruction. The BCDP presents 19 educationally sound and empirically supported principles for teaching basic concepts to young children (see Table C2). The Bracken concept list and instructional principles have become important in early childhood assessment and instruction internationally (Bracken, 1984, 1987, 1998b, 2006a, 2006b) because the BCDP integrates this available knowledge and a comprehensive list of basic language concepts into systematic classroom instruction (Bracken, 1987).

A comprehensive discussion of basic concepts is presented below by conceptual categories to bring uniformity to the teaching of basic concepts.

Colors

Colors are described as primary, secondary, or tertiary, and often are learned by young children in approximately that order. Primary colors are red, yellow, and blue. These colors are considered primary because no combination of colors is blended to produce a primary color. Secondary colors, on the other hand, are colors that result from blending two primary colors. As such, when the two primary colors yellow and blue are combined, they create the secondary color green; when red and blue are combined, they create purple; and when yellow and red are combined, they form orange. Orange, green, and purple then are secondary colors. When primary colors are blended with secondary colors, tertiary or intermediate colors are created, which vary depending on the proportions of each color added to the admixture (e.g., blue and green combined form the tertiary colors blue-green, heather, aquamarine, teal, and so on depending on the proportions of blue or green added).

Table C2
Instructional Principles for Teaching the Bracken Basic Concepts

	Bracken Instructional Principle
1	Language, examples, materials, and procedures used to teach concepts should be less complex than the concept being taught.
2	When concepts occur in pairs (e.g., up, down) or in series (e.g., before, just, after), maximize the meaningfulness of each concept by teaching all relevant concepts during the same lesson.
3	As much as possible, teach simple concepts, conceptual pairs, and series by using mnemonic strategies that facilitate understanding and enhance memory.
4	Concept generalizations should be taught initially by instruction with obvious examples of the concept and proceed to less obvious, more extreme examples. This instructional format should be followed with cases in which "nonexamples" are used to teach concept discrimination. Nonexamples should range initially from the apparent to relative nuances in later lessons.
5	Identify the characteristics that define the concept, distinguish which single dimension or group of characteristics are most salient, and provide instruction that initially emphasizes the most important characteristics, while minimizing the less important or irrelevant dimensions.
6	Instruction of polar concepts or concepts in a continuum should begin with the positive pole concept.
7	Concept pairs should be taught so that children identify positive examples as being *the concept* and negative examples (nonexamples) as *not being the concept*. Objects, for example, are either *tall* or *not tall*.
8	Once the positive pole concept is accurately described as *the concept* or *not the concept*, the child is taught that when it is *not the concept* it is the *negative pole concept* (e.g., if the object is *not tall*, then it is *short*).
9	When both polar concepts are learned, the teacher continues to display the logic that if it is *not the positive concept*, then it is *the negative concept* and if it is *not the negative concept*, then it is *the positive concept* (e.g., if the object is *not short*, then it is *tall*).
10	Consider the sequence in which concepts are acquired; the teacher should continually teach and assess to ensure that concept instruction is at the appropriate level.
11	School instruction should provide parents with a list of concepts and helpful suggestions as to how concepts can best be taught at home.
12	Conceptual lessons should elicit active participation and allow for multisensory instructional presentations.
13	Allow for overlearning in concept instruction by incorporating previously learned concepts in the lessons designed to teach new concepts.
14	Keep concept instructional sessions appropriately brief.
15	To ensure overlearning of concepts, allow for an adequate review of previously learned concepts before proceeding to new concepts.
16	Begin instructional sessions at a level that ensures success. Maintain an instructional difficulty level that guarantees continued success.
17	Structure conceptual instruction sessions so that each has an identifiable beginning and ending and objectives are clear.
18	Concepts should be taught in familiar situations in order to facilitate generalization.
19	To ensure a thorough understanding of basic concepts as instruction progresses, sessions should include conceptual combinations that are more complex than the instruction of single concepts.

Note. Adapted from Bracken (1987).

In addition to primary, secondary, and tertiary colors, there are the additional absolute colors of white and black. From a natural beam of light perspective, white is the combination of all primary colors, colors that can be separated into the full color spectrum comprised in a prism array. From an artificial, projected light beam perspective, white is the combination of red, green, and blue. Also from a light beam perspective, black is the total absence of color or as an extension, the absence of light. From a materials perspective, however, white is the absence of any color pigmentation and black is the combination of all colors. As such, white and black are contributors to the lightening or darkening of primary or secondary colors by degree of addition to the color admixture.

In combination, primary and secondary colors with the absolute colors of white and black added are universal colors for all people with normal color vision, and should constitute the educational basis for standards in color recognition and naming (Bracken, 1984, 1998b, 2006a, 2006b). Young children should be able to describe objects in terms of color, including the most basic primary and secondary colors, plus white and black.

Letters

Recognizing and naming the 26 letters of the alphabet appears to be the very foundation upon which reading preliteracy skills are developed. Developmental literature and the difficulty levels achieved among the Bracken concepts concur that children reliably recognize uppercase (i.e., capital) letters before they recognize lowercase letters, and later they are also able to name uppercase before lowercase letters, and later still they are able to reproduce the sounds that individual letters and consonant blends make.

The Bracken concept list includes the prereading concepts to include important phonemic awareness skills and abilities (i.e., letter and initial consonant blend sounds). Ideally, standards, curriculum, and instruction would systematically follow the developmental sequence of recognition followed by expression, including: (1) identifying uppercase letters, (2) identifying lowercase letters, (3) uppercase letter naming, (4) lowercase letter naming, (5) letter-sound production, and (6) initial consonant blend production.

Numbers/Counting

As with prereading skills, premath and early math skills have a fairly predictable developmental progression. Early on, young children develop a sense of quantity (e.g., more/less) and develop the ability to rote count without a one-to-one number/object correspondence. Later, young children learn to recognize numbers 1–5, followed by 6–9 and zero, and then double-digit numbers. Along the way, young children begin to count to 10 with one-to-one correspondence, and quickly they are on to counting to numbers greater than 100. Later still, young students learn to count by twos, fives, 10s, and so on.

Sizes/Comparisons

Sizes and comparative knowledge about size can be thought of in a number of ways, including considering objects in terms of their overall, three-dimensional size (e.g., big, small, large, little) or two-dimensional size, which may be depicted as vertical (e.g., tall, short) or horizontal (e.g., short, long), or diagonal. The developmental literature and item difficulty levels on the BBCS-R3 (Bracken, 2006a) generally support the assertion that students first learn concepts related to gross, three-dimensional size (e.g., big, small) before learning concepts related to two-dimensional size (e.g., tall, long). Students must be able to discern similarities and differences between the many attributes or dimensions of objects in our environment, including dimensions of relative size (e.g., same, equal, different),the more basic Bracken concepts of equal and unequal, and concepts in their most basic form (e.g., short), as well as in their comparative and superlative forms (i.e., shorter, shortest). Additional concepts that provide a more complete list of size concepts include unique contexts (e.g., deep/shallow, thin, thick) or employ comparative size language (e.g., same, not the same, equal, unequal, match, exact, similar).

Shapes

At the most basic level, shapes begin with lines, which may be straight, curvilinear (i.e., curved), or angled. Lines also may run in vertical, horizontal, or diagonal orientations.

Lines may be connected to create a whole object with two-dimensions (e.g., circle, square) or three-dimensions (e.g., sphere, cube). The comprehensive Bracken list includes many concepts such as those that define line nature (e.g., straight, curve, diagonal, angle), as well as a full range of two- and three-dimensional shapes (e.g., diamond, curve, angle, heart, checkmark, column, row, diagonal).

Direction/Position

Directions and locations (or positions) are relational concepts that describe the relative location or position of objects in space. From an early developmental orientation (i.e., non-perspective-taking orientation), objects are viewed in their locations from the perspective of the child (e.g., right is from the child's right-hand perspective); older children with the ability to take another's perspective can view locations from the orientation of others (e.g., opposing orientation where Sally's right is understood as the student's left). From a basic knowledge point of view, directional concepts are first learned from a self-perspective orientation and then later from another's perspective.

In addition to perspective, directions and position concepts by and large are represented most frequently as prepositions, but they also may include nouns (e.g., edge, corner). Early directional knowledge emphasizes a three-dimensional orientation from a self-perspective, and includes concepts that address vertical (e.g., above, below, up, down, under, over, high, low, top, bottom), horizontal (e.g., right, left, beside, next to, sideways), three-dimensional (e.g., around, through), internal/external (e.g., in, out, inside, outside, between), relative proximity (e.g., near, close, far), and the child's front or rear (e.g., front, back, forward, backward).

The Bracken concept list includes all of the aforementioned concepts plus many other related directional or positional concepts (e.g., falling, rising, together, apart, side, toward, away, apart, joined, together, height, length, opposite, level, space, moving, still, beginning, end, open, closed, on, off, upside down, following, ahead, behind). The Bracken Concept Development Program provides a comprehensive, logical extension of knowledge and a systematic treatment of the given universe of content

Self- and Social Awareness

The domain of self- and social awareness includes a wide array of personological and sociological knowledge, including affective feelings, health and physical condition, gender awareness, familial relationships, relative age, and social mores or correctness. As with academic content areas, students' sense of self and developing self-concepts are developmental in nature (Bracken, 1996).

The Bracken concept list includes the most comprehensive collection of concepts and knowledge in the area of self- and social-awareness. The Bracken concepts include conceptual knowledge associated with gender (e.g., male, female, boy, girl), familial relations (e.g., brother, sister, mother, father), age (e.g., old, young), health and physical awareness (e.g., tired, fatigued, rested, healthy, hurt, relaxing, sleepy, sick), affective state (e.g., happy, sad, crying, laughing, smiling, angry, afraid, excited, frowning, worried, curious), and social mores (e.g., right, wrong, correct, easy, difficult).

Texture/Material

From a developmental perspective, young children from birth begin to learn directly about their environments, including the attributes that define or characterize the objects in their environments. As infants crawl and toddlers toddle about and handle objects, they begin to develop an awareness of different textures (e.g., rough, hard, soft, smooth) and material characteristics or conditions (e.g., heavy, wet, dry, light). Parents begin to teach their children at very early ages the safety concept of hot and by comparison the polar opposite concept cold. Much later, children begin to learn what the objects in their environments are made of (e.g., wood, metal, glass, cloth) and they relate to the textures and material attributes that are consistent with each material (e.g., wood is hard; metal is heavy; glass is clear or sharp; cloth is soft, or sometimes rough). Finally, children learn about the manmade changing states of objects or materials (e.g., rough wood can be sanded smooth) or natural changing states of objects and materials (e.g., water can be found in various states, depending on temperature [i.e., liquid, solid, gas]). Such a comprehensive consideration and treatment of materials and textures as conceptual knowledge ensures that children are better able to use their five senses to identify, name, and discriminate between various object attributes, characteristics, and qualities at a young age.

The Bracken concept list includes conceptual knowledge across each of the five senses, except taste. Within the remaining four senses, however, the Bracken concepts comprehensively include knowledge of materials (e.g., cloth, wood), material attributes (e.g., wet, dry), material textures (e.g., rough, smooth, sharp), states of matter (e.g., liquid, solid, gas), temperature (e.g., hot, cold, boiling), sound (e.g., loud, quiet), and appearance (e.g., shiny, bright, clear, dull, dark, light).

Quantity

Quantitative knowledge in early childhood is part of, yet distinct from, students' understanding of numbers and counting. Knowledge of numbers and counting provides the foundation for much of the quantitative understanding that follows, but not always so. For example, it is obvious that virtually all young children have acquired the concept of more before they can identify numbers or count.

Quantitative concepts, then, represent the understanding of such conditions as part/whole (e.g., whole, part, piece), relative quantity (e.g., lots, few, many, nothing, none, every), volume (e.g., full, empty), comparatives (e.g., more than, less than), multiples (e.g., double, pair, couple, triple, dozen), fractions (e.g., half, third), currency (e.g., dime, nickel, quarter), and the use and understanding of mathematical signs (e.g., +, -, =). Quantity concepts provide young children with language that allows them to talk about numbers and counting in ways that communicate and generalize knowledge beyond the number of the objects being measured, weighed, counted, divided, distributed, or otherwise treated mathematically.

Time/Sequence

Because life progresses temporally, from birth to death, from morning to night, from breakfast to dinner, from new to old, from yesterday to tomorrow, young students quickly attend to the temporal patterns in their lives, even if they have not acquired the language to describe those patterns. In the domain of time/sequence, there is the obvious mathematical/quantitative nature of seriation (e.g., first, second, third) and frequency (e.g., once, twice) that also must be considered.

Knowledge of time and sequence, however, is more than just a quantitative component. Time and sequence also deal with students' knowledge and awareness of natural events (e.g., morning, daytime, night), temporal order of events (e.g., starting, before, after, over, finished), temporal absolutes (e.g., never, always), scheduling (e.g., early, late, next, arriving, leaving), speed (e.g., fast, slow), relative age (e.g., new, old, young, old), and descriptive temporal nuances (e.g., nearly, just, quit, waiting).

All of the previously mentioned time/sequence related concepts are found on the Bracken concept list.

Conclusions

The collective developmental and educational literature and the efforts of individual researchers have identified a comprehensive and unified combination of foundational knowledge that young children should know in order to ensure that all children possess a common knowledge base before entering advanced grades. This foundational knowledge is necessary to ensure that students have the language and understanding to learn about, talk about, and ask about content they learn in social studies, science, language arts, art, mathematics, and so on. This complete list of content and concepts constitute an extremely important foundation of knowledge.

If all young children possessed a thorough understanding of the basic concepts subsumed by these overarching categories of content that describe and comprise this universe of basic knowledge, all students would start their formal educations on a much more even footing. The knowledge base included in the list of Bracken concepts and the instructional principles provides parents and teachers a real, nonrhetorical, practical, and proven guide for placing a solid, common, and important foundation under all young students.

References

Bracken, B. A. (1984). *Bracken Basic Concept Scale.* San Antonio, TX: Harcourt Assessments.

Bracken, B. A. (1986). Incidence of basic concepts in the directions of five commonly used American tests of intelligence. *School Psychology International, 7,* 1–10.

Bracken, B. A. (1987). *Bracken Concept Development Program.* San Antonio: Harcourt Assessments.

Bracken, B. A. (1988). Rate and sequence of positive and negative pole concept acquisition. *Language, Speech, and Hearing Services in the Schools, 19,* 410–417.

Bracken, B. A. (1996). Clinical applications of a multidimensional, context-dependent model of self-concept. In B. A. Bracken (Ed.). *Handbook of self concept: Developmental, social, and clinical considerations* (pp. 463–505). New York: Wiley.

Bracken, B. A. (1998a). Basic concept acquisition and assessment: A celebration of our world's many dimensions. *Clinicians' Forum, 8*(2), 1, 7.

Bracken, B. A. (1998b). *Bracken Basic Concept Scale—Revised.* San Antonio, TX: Harcourt Assessments.

Bracken, B. A. (2006a). *Bracken Basic Concept Scale—Receptive Third Edition.* San Antonio, TX: Harcourt Assessments.

Bracken, B. A. (2006b). *Bracken Expressive.* San Antonio, TX: Harcourt Assessments.

Bracken, B. A., Barona, A., Bauermeister, J. J., Howell, K. K., Poggioli, L., & Puente, A. (1990). Multinational validation of the Bracken Basic Concept Scale. *Journal of School Psychology, 28,* 325–341.

Bracken, B. A., & Brown, E. F. (2008). Early identification of high-ability students: Clinical Assessment of Behavior. *Journal for the Education of the Gifted, 31,* 403–426.

Bracken, B. A., & Cato, L. A. (1986). Rate of conceptual development among deaf preschool and primary children as compared to a matched group of non-hearing impaired children. *Psychology in the Schools, 23,* 95–99.

Bracken, B. A., & Fouad, N. (1987). Spanish translation and validation of the Bracken Basic Concept Scale. *School Psychology Review, 16,* 94–102.

Breen, M. J. (1985). Concurrent validity of the Bracken Basic Concept Scale. *Journal of Psychoeducational Assessment, 3,* 37–44.

Center for Science, Mathematics, and Engineering Education. (1996). *National science education standards.* Washington, DC: National Academy Press.

Cummings, J. A., & Nelson, B. R. (1980). Basic concepts in oral directions of group achievement tests. *The Journal of Educational Research, 50,* 159–261.

Flanagan, D. P., Alfonso, V. C., Kaminer, T., & Rader, D. E. (1995). Incidence of basic concepts in the directions of new and recently revised American intelligence tests for preschool children. *School Psychology International, 16,* 345–364.

Frayer, D. A., Frederick, W. C., & Klausmeier, H. J. (1969). *A schema for testing the level of concept mastery.* Working paper from the Wisconsin Research and Development Center for Cognitive Learning, The University of Wisconsin.

Fowler, M. (1990). The diet cola test. *Science Scope, 13,* 32–34.

Holigan, M. (n.d.). *Making a terrarium.* Retrieved March 26, 2009, from http://michaelholigan.com/departments/TVShow/seg_tscript.asp?tsid=5739&text_type=S&text_page=1

Howell, K. K., & Bracken, B. A. (1992). Clinical utility of the Bracken Basic Concept Scale as a preschool intellectual screener: Comparison with the Stanford-Binet for Black children. *Journal of Clinical Child Psychology, 21,* 255–261.

Kaufman, A. S. (1978). The importance of basic concepts in the individual assessment of preschool children. *Journal of School Psychology, 16,* 208–211.

Kramer, S. P. (1987). *How to think like a scientist.* New York: HarperCollins.

McIntosh, D. E., Brown, M. L., & Ross, S. L. (1995). Relationship between the Bracken Basic Concept Scale and Differential Ability Scales with an at-risk sample of preschoolers. *Psychological Reports, 76,* 219–224.

McIntosh, D. E., Wayland, S. J., Gridley, B., & Barnes, L. L. B. (1995). Relationship between the Bracken Basic Concept Scale and the Differential Ability Scales with a preschool sample. *Journal of Psychoeducational Assessment, 13,* 39–48.

Novak, J., & Gowin, B. D. (1984). *Learning how to learn.* New York: Cambridge University Press.

Ortiz, E., & Kazilek, C. J. (2003). *Pocket seed experiment for the classroom and home.* Retrieved March 26, 2009, from http://askabiologist.asu.edu/expstuff/experiments/pocketseeds/Pocket_Packet_1.pdf

Panter, J. E. (2000). Validity of the Bracken Basic Concept Scale–Revised for predicting performance on the Metropolitan Readiness Test–Sixth Edition. *Journal of Psychoeducational Assessment,* 18, 104–110.

Panter, J. E., & Bracken, B. A. (2000). Promoting school readiness. In K. M. Minke & G. G. Bear (Eds.), *Preventing school problems—Promoting school success: Strategies and programs that work* (pp. 101–142). Bethesda, MD: NASP.

Panter, J. E., & Bracken, B. A. (in press). Validity of the Bracken School Readiness Assessment for predicting first grade readiness. *Psychology in the Schools.*

Rhyner, P. M., & Bracken, B. A. (1988). Concurrent validity of the Bracken Basic Concept Scale with language and intelligence measures. *Journal of Communication Disorders, 21,* 479–489.

Rutherford, F. J., & Ahlgren, A. (1991). *Science for all Americans.* New York: Oxford University Press.

Scholastic. (1996). *Scholastic children's dictionary.* New York: Author.

Sher, B. T. (2004). Systems. In J. VanTassel-Baska (Ed.), *Science key concepts.* Williamsburg, VA: Center for Gifted Education, The College of William and Mary.

Stebbins, M. S., & McIntosh, D. E. (1996). Decision-making utility of the Bracken Basic Concept Scale in identifying at-risk preschoolers. *School Psychology International, 17,* 293–303.

Sterner, A. G., & McCallum, R. S. (1988). Relationship of the Gesell Developmental Exam and the Bracken Basic Concept Scale to academic achievement. *Journal of School Psychology, 26,* 297–300.

Taba, H. (1962). *Curriculum: Theory and practice.* New York: Harcourt, Brace.

VanTassel-Baska, J. (1986). Effective curriculum and instructional models for talented students. *Gifted Child Quarterly, 30,* 164–169.

VanTassel-Baska, J., & Little, C. (Eds.). (2003). *Content-based curriculum for gifted learners.* Waco, TX: Prufrock Press.

Wilson, P. (2004). A preliminary investigation of an early intervention program: Examining the intervention effectiveness of the Bracken Concept Development Program and the Bracken Basic Concept Scale–Revised with Head Start students. *Psychology in the Schools, 41,* 301–311.